Supplement To

Illinois

Court Rules and

Procedure

Volume II – Federal

September 2015

NOTICE

This Supplement should be affixed with the peel-off adhesive to the inside back cover of your *Illinois Court Rules and Procedure, Volume II – Federal, 2015* pamphlet.

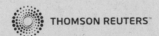
THOMSON REUTERS

Material #41847842

© 2015 Thomson Reuters

Copyright is not claimed as to any part of the original work prepared by a United States Government officer or employee as part of that person's official duties.

This publication was created to provide you with accurate and authoritative information concerning the subject matter covered; however, this publication was not necessarily prepared by persons licensed to practice law in a particular jurisdiction. The publisher is not engaged in rendering legal or other professional advice and this publication is not a substitute for the advice of an attorney. If you require legal or other expert advice, you should seek the services of a competent attorney or other professional.

West's and Westlaw are registered in the U.S. Patent and Trademark Office.

PREFACE

This Supplement contains amendments received through August 1, 2015.

THE PUBLISHER

September 2015

TABLE OF CONTENTS

FEDERAL
RULES OF CIVIL PROCEDURE
FOR THE
UNITED STATES DISTRICT COURTS

Including Amendments Effective December 1, 2015,
Absent Contrary Congressional Action

TITLE I. SCOPE OF RULES; FORM OF ACTION

RULE 1. SCOPE AND PURPOSE

[Text of Rule 1 effective until December 1, 2015, absent contrary Congressional action.]

These rules govern the procedure in all civil actions and proceedings in the United States district courts, except as stated in Rule 81. They should be construed and administered to secure the just, speedy, and inexpensive determination of every action and proceeding.

[Text of Rule 1 effective December 1, 2015, absent contrary Congressional action.]

These rules govern the procedure in all civil actions and proceedings in the United States district courts, except as stated in Rule 81. They should be construed, administered, and employed by the court and the parties to secure the just, speedy, and inexpensive determination of every action and proceeding.

(Amended December 29, 1948, effective October 20, 1949; February 28, 1966, effective July 1, 1966; April 22, 1993, effective December 1, 1993; April 30, 2007, effective December 1, 2007; April 29, 2015, effective December 1, 2015, absent contrary Congressional action.)

TITLE II. COMMENCING AN ACTION; SERVICE OF PROCESS, PLEADINGS, MOTIONS, AND ORDERS

RULE 4. SUMMONS

(a) Contents; Amendments.

  (1) *Contents.* A summons must:

    (A) name the court and the parties;

    (B) be directed to the defendant;

    (C) state the name and address of the plaintiff's attorney or—if unrepresented—of the plaintiff;

    (D) state the time within which the defendant must appear and defend;

    (E) notify the defendant that a failure to appear and defend will result in a default judgment against the defendant for the relief demanded in the complaint;

    (F) be signed by the clerk; and

    (G) bear the court's seal.

  (2) *Amendments.* The court may permit a summons to be amended.

(b) Issuance. On or after filing the complaint, the plaintiff may present a summons to the clerk for signature and seal. If the summons is properly completed, the clerk must sign, seal, and issue it to the plaintiff for service on the defendant. A summons—or a copy of a summons that is addressed to multiple defendants—must be issued for each defendant to be served.

(c) Service.

    (1) *In General.* A summons must be served with a copy of the complaint. The plaintiff is responsible for having the summons and complaint served within the time allowed by Rule 4(m) and must furnish the necessary copies to the person who makes service.

    (2) *By Whom.* Any person who is at least 18 years old and not a party may serve a summons and complaint.

    (3) *By a Marshal or Someone Specially Appointed.* At the plaintiff's request, the court may order that service be made by a United States marshal or deputy marshal or by a person specially appointed by the court. The court must so order if the plaintiff is authorized to proceed in forma pauperis under 28 U.S.C. § 1915 or as a seaman under 28 U.S.C. § 1916.

[Text of subdivision (d) effective until December 1, 2015, absent contrary Congressional action.]

(d) Waiving Service.

    (1) *Requesting a Waiver.* An individual, corporation, or association that is subject to service under Rule 4(e), (f), or (h) has a duty to avoid unnecessary expenses of serving the summons. The plaintiff may notify such a defendant that an action has been commenced and request that the defendant waive service of a summons. The notice and request must:

    (A) be in writing and be addressed:

      (i) to the individual defendant; or

      (ii) for a defendant subject to service under Rule 4(h), to an officer, a managing or general agent, or any other agent authorized by appointment or by law to receive service of process;

    (B) name the court where the complaint was filed;

    (C) be accompanied by a copy of the complaint, two copies of a waiver form, and a prepaid means for returning the form;

    (D) inform the defendant, using text prescribed in Form 5, of the consequences of waiving and not waiving service;

    (E) state the date when the request is sent;

    (F) give the defendant a reasonable time of at least 30 days after the request was sent—or at least 60 days if sent to the defendant outside any judicial district of the United States—to return the waiver; and

    (G) be sent by first-class mail or other reliable means.

    (2) *Failure to Waive.* If a defendant located within the United States fails, without good cause, to sign and return a waiver requested by a plaintiff located within the United States, the court must impose on the defendant:

    (A) the expenses later incurred in making service; and

    (B) the reasonable expenses, including attorney's fees, of any motion required to collect those service expenses.

    (3) *Time to Answer After a Waiver.* A defendant who, before being served with process, timely returns a waiver need not serve an answer to the complaint until 60 days after the request was sent—or until 90 days after it was sent to the defendant outside any judicial district of the United States.

    (4) *Results of Filing a Waiver.* When the plaintiff files a waiver, proof of service is not required and these rules apply as if a summons and complaint had been served at the time of filing the waiver.

    (5) *Jurisdiction and Venue Not Waived.* Waiving service of a summons does not waive any objection to personal jurisdiction or to venue.

[Text of subdivision (d) effective December 1, 2015, absent contrary Congressional action.]

(d) Waiving Service.

    (1) *Requesting a Waiver.* An individual, corporation, or association that is subject to service under Rule 4(e), (f),

or (h) has a duty to avoid unnecessary expenses of serving the summons. The plaintiff may notify such a defendant that an action has been commenced and request that the defendant waive service of a summons. The notice and request must:

(A) be in writing and be addressed:

  (i) to the individual defendant; or

  (ii) for a defendant subject to service under Rule 4(h), to an officer, a managing or general agent, or any other agent authorized by appointment or by law to receive service of process;

(B) name the court where the complaint was filed;

(C) be accompanied by a copy of the complaint, 2 copies of the waiver form appended to this Rule 4, and a prepaid means for returning the form;

(D) inform the defendant, using the form appended to this Rule 4, of the consequences of waiving and not waiving service;

(E) state the date when the request is sent;

(F) give the defendant a reasonable time of at least 30 days after the request was sent—or at least 60 days if sent to the defendant outside any judicial district of the United States—to return the waiver; and

(G) be sent by first-class mail or other reliable means.

(2) *Failure to Waive.* If a defendant located within the United States fails, without good cause, to sign and return a waiver requested by a plaintiff located within the United States, the court must impose on the defendant:

(A) the expenses later incurred in making service; and

(B) the reasonable expenses, including attorney's fees, of any motion required to collect those service expenses.

(3) *Time to Answer After a Waiver.* A defendant who, before being served with process, timely returns a waiver need not serve an answer to the complaint until 60 days after the request was sent—or until 90 days after it was sent to the defendant outside any judicial district of the United States.

(4) *Results of Filing a Waiver.* When the plaintiff files a waiver, proof of service is not required and these rules apply as if a summons and complaint had been served at the time of filing the waiver.

(5) *Jurisdiction and Venue Not Waived.* Waiving service of a summons does not waive any objection to personal jurisdiction or to venue.

(e) **Serving an Individual Within a Judicial District of the United States.** Unless federal law provides otherwise, an individual—other than a minor, an incompetent person, or a person whose waiver has been filed—may be served in a judicial district of the United States by:

(1) following state law for serving a summons in an action brought in courts of general jurisdiction in the state where the district court is located or where service is made; or

(2) doing any of the following:

(A) delivering a copy of the summons and of the complaint to the individual personally;

(B) leaving a copy of each at the individual's dwelling or usual place of abode with someone of suitable age and discretion who resides there; or

(C) delivering a copy of each to an agent authorized by appointment or by law to receive service of process.

(f) **Serving an Individual in a Foreign Country.** Unless federal law provides otherwise, an individual—other than a minor, an incompetent person, or a person whose waiver has been filed—may be served at a place not within any judicial district of the United States:

(1) by any internationally agreed means of service that is reasonably calculated to give notice, such as those authorized by the Hague Convention on the Service Abroad of Judicial and Extrajudicial Documents;

(2) if there is no internationally agreed means, or if an international agreement allows but does not specify other means, by a method that is reasonably calculated to give notice:

(A) as prescribed by the foreign country's law for service in that country in an action in its courts of general jurisdiction;

(B) as the foreign authority directs in response to a letter rogatory or letter of request; or

(C) unless prohibited by the foreign country's law, by:

  (i) delivering a copy of the summons and of the complaint to the individual personally; or

  (ii) using any form of mail that the clerk addresses and sends to the individual and that requires a signed receipt; or

(3) by other means not prohibited by international agreement, as the court orders.

(g) Serving a Minor or an Incompetent Person. A minor or an incompetent person in a judicial district of the United States must be served by following state law for serving a summons or like process on such a defendant in an action brought in the courts of general jurisdiction of the state where service is made. A minor or an incompetent person who is not within any judicial district of the United States must be served in the manner prescribed by Rule 4(f)(2)(A), (f)(2)(B), or (f)(3).

(h) Serving a Corporation, Partnership, or Association. Unless federal law provides otherwise or the defendant's waiver has been filed, a domestic or foreign corporation, or a partnership or other unincorporated association that is subject to suit under a common name, must be served:

(1) in a judicial district of the United States:

  (A) in the manner prescribed by Rule 4(e)(1) for serving an individual; or

  (B) by delivering a copy of the summons and of the complaint to an officer, a managing or general agent, or any other agent authorized by appointment or by law to receive service of process and—if the agent is one authorized by statute and the statute so requires—by also mailing a copy of each to the defendant; or

(2) at a place not within any judicial district of the United States, in any

manner prescribed by Rule 4(f) for serving an individual, except personal delivery under (f)(2)(C)(i).

(i) Serving the United States and Its Agencies, Corporations, Officers, or Employees.

(1) *United States.* To serve the United States, a party must:

  (A)(i) deliver a copy of the summons and of the complaint to the United States attorney for the district where the action is brought—or to an assistant United States attorney or clerical employee whom the United States attorney designates in a writing filed with the court clerk—or

  (ii) send a copy of each by registered or certified mail to the civil-process clerk at the United States attorney's office;

  (B) send a copy of each by registered or certified mail to the Attorney General of the United States at Washington, D.C.; and

  (C) if the action challenges an order of a nonparty agency or officer of the United States, send a copy of each by registered or certified mail to the agency or officer.

(2) *Agency; Corporation; Officer or Employee Sued in an Official Capacity.* To serve a United States agency or corporation, or a United States officer or employee sued only in an official capacity, a party must serve the United States and also send a copy of the summons and of the complaint by registered or certified mail to the agency, corporation, officer, or employee.

(3) *Officer or Employee Sued Individually.* To serve a United States officer or employee sued in an individual capacity for an act or omission occurring in connection with duties performed on the United States' behalf (whether or not the officer or employee is also sued in an official capacity), a party must serve the United States and also serve the officer or employee under Rule 4(e), (f), or (g).

4

(4) *Extending Time.* The court must allow a party a reasonable time to cure its failure to:

(A) serve a person required to be served under Rule 4(i)(2), if the party has served either the United States attorney or the Attorney General of the United States; or

(B) serve the United States under Rule 4(i)(3), if the party has served the United States officer or employee.

(j) Serving a Foreign, State, or Local Government.

(1) *Foreign State.* A foreign state or its political subdivision, agency, or instrumentality must be served in accordance with 28 U.S.C. § 1608.

(2) *State or Local Government.* A state, a municipal corporation, or any other state-created governmental organization that is subject to suit must be served by:

(A) delivering a copy of the summons and of the complaint to its chief executive officer; or

(B) serving a copy of each in the manner prescribed by that state's law for serving a summons or like process on such a defendant.

(k) Territorial Limits of Effective Service.

(1) *In General.* Serving a summons or filing a waiver of service establishes personal jurisdiction over a defendant:

(A) who is subject to the jurisdiction of a court of general jurisdiction in the state where the district court is located;

(B) who is a party joined under Rule 14 or 19 and is served within a judicial district of the United States and not more than 100 miles from where the summons was issued; or

(C) when authorized by a federal statute.

(2) *Federal Claim Outside State–Court Jurisdiction.* For a claim that arises under federal law, serving a summons or filing a waiver of service establishes personal jurisdiction over a defendant if:

(A) the defendant is not subject to jurisdiction in any state's courts of general jurisdiction; and

(B) exercising jurisdiction is consistent with the United States Constitution and laws.

(*l*) Proving Service.

(1) *Affidavit Required.* Unless service is waived, proof of service must be made to the court. Except for service by a United States marshal or deputy marshal, proof must be by the server's affidavit.

(2) *Service Outside the United States.* Service not within any judicial district of the United States must be proved as follows:

(A) if made under Rule 4(f)(1), as provided in the applicable treaty or convention; or

(B) if made under Rule 4(f)(2) or (f)(3), by a receipt signed by the addressee, or by other evidence satisfying the court that the summons and complaint were delivered to the addressee.

(3) *Validity of Service; Amending Proof.* Failure to prove service does not affect the validity of service. The court may permit proof of service to be amended.

[Text of subdivision (m) effective until December 1, 2015, absent contrary Congressional action.]

(m) Time Limit for Service. If a defendant is not served within 120 days after the complaint is filed, the court— on motion or on its own after notice to the plaintiff—must dismiss the action without prejudice against that defendant or order that service be made within a specified time. But if the plaintiff shows good cause for the failure, the court must extend the time for service for an appropriate period. This subdivision (m) does not apply to service in a foreign country under Rule 4(f) or 4(j)(1).

[Text of subdivision (m) effective December 1, 2015, absent contrary Congressional action.]

(m) Time Limit for Service. If a defendant is not served within 90 days after the complaint is filed, the court — on motion or on its own after notice to the plaintiff — must dismiss the action

5

without prejudice against that defendant or order that service be made within a specified time. But if the plaintiff shows good cause for the failure, the court must extend the time for service for an appropriate period. This subdivision (m) does not apply to service in a foreign country under Rule 4(f) or 4(j)(1) or to service of a notice under Rule 71.1(d)(3)(A).

(n) Asserting Jurisdiction over Property or Assets.

(1) *Federal Law.* The court may assert jurisdiction over property if authorized by a federal statute. Notice to claimants of the property must be given as provided in the statute or by serving a summons under this rule.

(2) *State Law.* On a showing that personal jurisdiction over a defendant cannot be obtained in the district where the action is brought by reasonable efforts to serve a summons under this rule, the court may assert jurisdiction over the defendant's assets found in the district. Jurisdiction is acquired by seizing the assets under the circumstances and in the manner provided by state law in that district.

[Text of former Form 5 effective December 1, 2015, absent contrary Congressional action.]

Rule 4   Notice of a Lawsuit and Request to Waive Service of Summons.

(Caption)

To (*name the defendant or — if the defendant is a corporation, partnership, or association — name an officer or agent authorized to receive service*):

Why are you getting this?

A lawsuit has been filed against you, or the entity you represent, in this court under the number shown above. A copy of the complaint is attached.

This is not a summons, or an official notice from the court. It is a request that, to avoid expenses, you waive formal service of a summons by signing and returning the enclosed waiver. To avoid these expenses,

you must return the signed waiver within (*give at least 30 days or at least 60 days if the defendant is outside any judicial district of the United States*) from the date shown below, which is the date this notice was sent. Two copies of the waiver form are enclosed, along with a stamped, self-addressed envelope or other prepaid means for returning one copy. You may keep the other copy.

What happens next?

If you return the signed waiver, I will file it with the court. The action will then proceed as if you had been served on the date the waiver is filed, but no summons will be served on you and you will have 60 days from the date this notice is sent (see the date below) to answer the complaint (or 90 days if this notice is sent to you outside any judicial district of the United States).

If you do not return the signed waiver within the time indicated, I will arrange to have the summons and complaint served on you. And I will ask the court to require you, or the entity you represent, to pay the expenses of making service.

Please read the enclosed statement about the duty to avoid unnecessary expenses.

I certify that this request is being sent to you on the date below.

Date: _____

_____
(Signature of the attorney or unrepresented party)

_____
(Printed name)

_____
(Address)

_____
(E–mail address)

_____
(Telephone number)

[Text of former Form 6 effective December 1, 2015, absent contrary Congressional action.]

Rule 4   Waiver of the Service of Summons.

(Caption)

To (*name the plaintiff's attorney or the unrepresented plaintiff*):

I have received your request to waive service of a summons in this action along with a copy of the complaint, two copies of this waiver form, and a prepaid means of returning one signed copy of the form to you.

I, or the entity I represent, agree to save the expense of serving a summons and complaint in this case.

I understand that I, or the entity I represent, will keep all defenses or objections to the lawsuit, the court's jurisdiction, and the venue of the action, but that I waive any objections to the absence of a summons or of service.

I also understand that I, or the entity I represent, must file and serve an answer or a motion under Rule 12 within 60 days from _____, the date when this request was sent (or 90 days if it was sent outside the United States). If I fail to do so, a default judgment will be entered against me or the entity I represent.

Date: _____

_____
(Signature of the attorney
or unrepresented party)

_____
(Printed name)

_____
(Address)

_____
(E–mail address)

_____
(Telephone number)

(Attach the following)
**Duty to Avoid Unnecessary Expenses
of Serving a Summons**

Rule 4 of the Federal Rules of Civil Procedure requires certain defendants to cooperate in saving unnecessary expenses of serving a summons and complaint. A defendant who is located in the United States and who fails to return a signed waiver of service requested by a plaintiff located in the United States will be required to pay the expenses of service, unless the defendant shows good cause for the failure.

"Good cause" does not include a belief that the lawsuit is groundless, or that it has been brought in an improper venue, or that the court has no jurisdiction over this matter or over the defendant or the defendant's property.

If the waiver is signed and returned, you can still make these and all other defenses and objections, but you cannot object to the absence of a summons or of service.

If you waive service, then you must, within the time specified on the waiver form, serve an answer or a motion under Rule 12 on the plaintiff and file a copy with the court. By signing and returning the waiver form, you are allowed more time to respond than if a summons had been served.

(Amended January 21, 1963, effective July 1, 1963; February 28, 1966, effective July 1, 1966; April 29, 1980, effective August 1, 1980; amended by Pub.L. 97-462, § 2, January 12, 1983, 96 Stat. 2527, effective 45 days after January 12, 1983; amended March 2, 1987, effective August 1, 1987; April 22, 1993, effective December 1, 1993; April 17, 2000, effective December 1, 2000; April 30, 2007, effective December 1, 2007; April 29, 2015, effective December 1, 2015, absent contrary Congressional action.)

TITLE III.   PLEADINGS AND MOTIONS

RULE 16.   PRETRIAL CONFERENCES; SCHEDULING; MANAGEMENT

(a) **Purposes of a Pretrial Conference.** In any action, the court may order the attorneys and any unrepresented parties to appear for one or more pretrial conferences for such purposes as:

(1) expediting disposition of the action;

(2) establishing early and continuing control so that the case will not be protracted because of lack of management;

(3) discouraging wasteful pretrial activities;

(4) improving the quality of the trial through more thorough preparation; and

(5) facilitating settlement.

[Text of subdivision (b) effective until December 1, 2015, absent contrary Congressional action.]

(b) **Scheduling.**

(1) *Scheduling Order.* Except in categories of actions exempted by local rule, the district judge—or a magistrate judge when authorized by local rule—must issue a scheduling order:

(A) after receiving the parties' report under Rule 26(f); or

(B) after consulting with the parties' attorneys and any unrepresented parties at a scheduling conference or by telephone, mail, or other means.

(2) *Time to Issue.* The judge must issue the scheduling order as soon as practicable, but in any event within the earlier of 120 days after any defendant has been served with the complaint or 90 days after any defendant has appeared.

(3) *Contents of the Order.*

(A) *Required Contents.* The scheduling order must limit the time to join other parties, amend the pleadings, complete discovery, and file motions.

(B) *Permitted Contents.* The scheduling order may:

(i) modify the timing of disclosures under Rules 26(a) and 26(e)(1);

(ii) modify the extent of discovery;

(iii) provide for disclosure or discovery of electronically stored information;

(iv) include any agreements the parties reach for asserting claims of privilege or of protection as trial-preparation material after information is produced;

(v) set dates for pretrial conferences and for trial; and

(vi) include other appropriate matters.

(4) *Modifying a Schedule.* A schedule may be modified only for good cause and with the judge's consent.

[Text of subdivision (b) effective December 1, 2015, absent contrary Congressional action.]

(b) Scheduling.

(1) *Scheduling Order.* Except in categories of actions exempted by local rule, the district judge—or a magistrate

judge when authorized by local rule—must issue a scheduling order:

(A) after receiving the parties' report under Rule 26(f); or

(B) after consulting with the parties' attorneys and any unrepresented parties at a scheduling conference.

(2) *Time to Issue.* The judge must issue the scheduling order as soon as practicable, but unless the judge finds good cause for delay, the judge must issue it within the earlier of 90 days after any defendant has been served with the complaint or 60 days after any defendant has appeared.

(3) *Contents of the Order.*

(A) *Required Contents.* The scheduling order must limit the time to join other parties, amend the pleadings, complete discovery, and file motions.

(B) *Permitted Contents.* The scheduling order may:

(i) modify the timing of disclosures under Rules 26(a) and 26(e)(1);

(ii) modify the extent of discovery;

(iii) provide for disclosure, discovery, or preservation of electronically stored information;

(iv) include any agreements the parties reach for asserting claims of privilege or of protection as trial-preparation material after information is produced, including agreements reached under Federal Rule of Evidence 502;

(v) direct that before moving for an order relating to discovery, the movant must request a conference with the court;

(vi) set dates for pretrial conferences and for trial; and

(vii) include other appropriate matters.

(4) *Modifying a Schedule.* A schedule may be modified only for good cause and with the judge's consent.

(c) Attendance and Matters for Consideration at a Pretrial Conference.

(1) *Attendance.* A represented party must authorize at least one of its attorneys to make stipulations and admissions about all matters that can reasonably be anticipated for discus-

8

sion at a pretrial conference. If appropriate, the court may require that a party or its representative be present or reasonably available by other means to consider possible settlement.

(2) *Matters for Consideration.* At any pretrial conference, the court may consider and take appropriate action on the following matters:

(A) formulating and simplifying the issues, and eliminating frivolous claims or defenses;

(B) amending the pleadings if necessary or desirable;

(C) obtaining admissions and stipulations about facts and documents to avoid unnecessary proof, and ruling in advance on the admissibility of evidence;

(D) avoiding unnecessary proof and cumulative evidence, and limiting the use of testimony under Federal Rule of Evidence 702;

(E) determining the appropriateness and timing of summary adjudication under Rule 56;

(F) controlling and scheduling discovery, including orders affecting disclosures and discovery under Rule 26 and Rules 29 through 37;

(G) identifying witnesses and documents, scheduling the filing and exchange of any pretrial briefs, and setting dates for further conferences and for trial;

(H) referring matters to a magistrate judge or a master;

(I) settling the case and using special procedures to assist in resolving the dispute when authorized by statute or local rule;

(J) determining the form and content of the pretrial order;

(K) disposing of pending motions;

(L) adopting special procedures for managing potentially difficult or protracted actions that may involve complex issues, multiple parties, difficult legal questions, or unusual proof problems;

(M) ordering a separate trial under Rule 42(b) of a claim, counterclaim, crossclaim, third-party claim, or particular issue;

(N) ordering the presentation of evidence early in the trial on a manageable issue that might, on the evidence, be the basis for a judgment as a matter of law under Rule 50(a) or a judgment on partial findings under Rule 52(c);

(O) establishing a reasonable limit on the time allowed to present evidence; and

(P) facilitating in other ways the just, speedy, and inexpensive disposition of the action.

(d) **Pretrial Orders.** After any conference under this rule, the court should issue an order reciting the action taken. This order controls the course of the action unless the court modifies it.

(e) **Final Pretrial Conference and Orders.** The court may hold a final pretrial conference to formulate a trial plan, including a plan to facilitate the admission of evidence. The conference must be held as close to the start of trial as is reasonable, and must be attended by at least one attorney who will conduct the trial for each party and by any unrepresented party. The court may modify the order issued after a final pretrial conference only to prevent manifest injustice.

(f) **Sanctions.**

(1) *In General.* On motion or on its own, the court may issue any just orders, including those authorized by Rule 37(b)(2)(A)(ii)-(vii), if a party or its attorney:

(A) fails to appear at a scheduling or other pretrial conference;

(B) is substantially unprepared to participate—or does not participate in good faith—in the conference; or

(C) fails to obey a scheduling or other pretrial order.

(2) *Imposing Fees and Costs.* Instead of or in addition to any other sanction, the court must order the party, its attorney, or both to pay the reasonable expenses—including attorney's fees—incurred because of any noncompliance with this rule, unless the noncompliance was substantially justified or other circumstances make an award of expenses unjust.

(Amended April 28, 1983, effective August 1, 1983; March 2, 1987, effective August 1, 1987; April 22, 1993, effective December 1, 1993; April 12, 2006, effective December 1, 2006; April 30, 2007, effective December 1, 2007; April 29, 2015, effective December 1, 2015, absent contrary Congressional action.)

TITLE V.   DISCLOSURES AND DISCOVERY

RULE 26.   DUTY TO DISCLOSE; GENERAL PROVISIONS GOVERNING DISCOVERY

(a) Required Disclosures.

(1) *Initial Disclosure.*

(A) *In General.* Except as exempted by Rule 26(a)(1)(B) or as otherwise stipulated or ordered by the court, a party must, without awaiting a discovery request, provide to the other parties:

(i) the name and, if known, the address and telephone number of each individual likely to have discoverable information—along with the subjects of that information—that the disclosing party may use to support its claims or defenses, unless the use would be solely for impeachment;

(ii) a copy—or a description by category and location—of all documents, electronically stored information, and tangible things that the disclosing party has in its possession, custody, or control and may use to support its claims or defenses, unless the use would be solely for impeachment;

(iii) a computation of each category of damages claimed by the disclosing party—who must also make available for inspection and copying as under Rule 34 the documents or other evidentiary material, unless privileged or protected from disclosure, on which each computation is based, including materials bearing on the nature and extent of injuries suffered; and

(iv) for inspection and copying as under Rule 34, any insurance agreement under which an insurance business may be liable to satisfy all or part of a possible judgment in the action or to indemnify or reimburse for payments made to satisfy the judgment.

(B) *Proceedings Exempt from Initial Disclosure.* The following proceedings are exempt from initial disclosure:

(i) an action for review on an administrative record;

(ii) a forfeiture action in rem arising from a federal statute;

(iii) a petition for habeas corpus or any other proceeding to challenge a criminal conviction or sentence;

(iv) an action brought without an attorney by a person in the custody of the United States, a state, or a state subdivision;

(v) an action to enforce or quash an administrative summons or subpoena;

(vi) an action by the United States to recover benefit payments;

(vii) an action by the United States to collect on a student loan guaranteed by the United States;

(viii) a proceeding ancillary to a proceeding in another court; and

(ix) an action to enforce an arbitration award.

(C) *Time for Initial Disclosures—In General.* A party must make the initial disclosures at or within 14 days after the parties' Rule 26(f) conference unless a different time is set by stipulation or court order, or unless a party objects during the conference that initial disclosures are not appropriate in this action and states the objection in the proposed discovery plan. In ruling on the objection, the court must determine what disclosures, if any, are to be made and must set the time for disclosure.

(D) *Time for Initial Disclosures—For Parties Served or Joined Later.* A party that is first served or otherwise joined after the Rule 26(f) conference must make the initial disclosures within 30 days after being served or joined, unless a different time is set by stipulation or court order.

(E) *Basis for Initial Disclosure; Unacceptable Excuses.* A party must make its initial disclosures based on the information then reasonably available to it. A party is not excused from making its disclosures because it has not fully investigated the case or because it challenges the sufficiency of another party's disclosures or because another party has not made its disclosures.

(2) *Disclosure of Expert Testimony.*

(A) *In General.* In addition to the disclosures required by Rule 26(a)(1), a party must disclose to the other parties the identity of any witness it may use at trial to present evidence under Federal Rule of Evidence 702, 703, or 705.

(B) *Witnesses Who Must Provide a Written Report.* Unless otherwise stipulated or ordered by the court, this disclosure must be accompanied by a written report—prepared and signed by the witness—if the witness is one retained or specially employed to provide expert testimony in the case or one whose duties as the party's employee regularly involve giving expert testimony. The report must contain:

(i) a complete statement of all opinions the witness will express and the basis and reasons for them;

(ii) the facts or data considered by the witness in forming them;

(iii) any exhibits that will be used to summarize or support them;

(iv) the witness's qualifications, including a list of all publications authored in the previous 10 years;

(v) a list of all other cases in which, during the previous 4 years, the witness testified as an expert at trial or by deposition; and

(vi) a statement of the compensation to be paid for the study and testimony in the case.

(C) *Witnesses Who Do Not Provide a Written Report.* Unless otherwise stipulated or ordered by the court, if the witness is not required to provide a written report, this disclosure must state:

(i) the subject matter on which the witness is expected to present evidence under Federal Rule of Evidence 702, 703, or 705; and

(ii) a summary of the facts and opinions to which the witness is expected to testify.

(D) *Time to Disclose Expert Testimony.* A party must make these disclosures at the times and in the sequence that the court orders. Absent a stipulation or a court order, the disclosures must be made:

(i) at least 90 days before the date set for trial or for the case to be ready for trial; or

(ii) if the evidence is intended solely to contradict or rebut evidence on the same subject matter identified by another party under Rule 26(a)(2)(B) or (C), within 30 days after the other party's disclosure.

(E) *Supplementing the Disclosure.* The parties must supplement these disclosures when required under Rule 26(e).

(3) *Pretrial Disclosures.*

(A) *In General.* In addition to the disclosures required by Rule 26(a)(1) and (2), a party must provide to the other parties and promptly file

11

the following information about the evidence that it may present at trial other than solely for impeachment:

  (i) the name and, if not previously provided, the address and telephone number of each witness— separately identifying those the party expects to present and those it may call if the need arises;

  (ii) the designation of those witnesses whose testimony the party expects to present by deposition and, if not taken stenographically, a transcript of the pertinent parts of the deposition; and

  (iii) an identification of each document or other exhibit, including summaries of other evidence— separately identifying those items the party expects to offer and those it may offer if the need arises.

(B) *Time for Pretrial Disclosures; Objections.* Unless the court orders otherwise, these disclosures must be made at least 30 days before trial. Within 14 days after they are made, unless the court sets a different time, a party may serve and promptly file a list of the following objections: any objections to the use under Rule 32(a) of a deposition designated by another party under Rule 26(a)(3)(A)(ii); and any objection, together with the grounds for it, that may be made to the admissibility of materials identified under Rule 26(a)(3)(A)(iii). An objection not so made—except for one under Federal Rule of Evidence 402 or 403—is waived unless excused by the court for good cause.

(4) *Form of Disclosures.* Unless the court orders otherwise, all disclosures under Rule 26(a) must be in writing, signed, and served.

[Text of subdivision (b) effective until December 1, 2015, absent contrary Congressional action.]

(b) Discovery Scope and Limits.

  (1) *Scope in General.* Unless otherwise limited by court order, the scope of discovery is as follows: Parties may obtain discovery regarding any non-privileged matter that is relevant to any party's claim or defense—including the existence, description, nature, custody, condition, and location of any documents or other tangible things and the identity and location of persons who know of any discoverable matter. For good cause, the court may order discovery of any matter relevant to the subject matter involved in the action. Relevant information need not be admissible at the trial if the discovery appears reasonably calculated to lead to the discovery of admissible evidence. All discovery is subject to the limitations imposed by Rule 26(b)(2)(C).

  (2) *Limitations on Frequency and Extent.*

    (A) *When Permitted.* By order, the court may alter the limits in these rules on the number of depositions and interrogatories or on the length of depositions under Rule 30. By order or local rule, the court may also limit the number of requests under Rule 36.

    (B) *Specific Limitations on Electronically Stored Information.* A party need not provide discovery of electronically stored information from sources that the party identifies as not reasonably accessible because of undue burden or cost. On motion to compel discovery or for a protective order, the party from whom discovery is sought must show that the information is not reasonably accessible because of undue burden or cost. If that showing is made, the court may nonetheless order discovery from such sources if the requesting party shows good cause, considering the limitations of Rule 26(b)(2)(C). The court may specify conditions for the discovery.

    (C) *When Required.* On motion or on its own, the court must limit the frequency or extent of discovery otherwise allowed by these rules or by local rule if it determines that:

(i) the discovery sought is unreasonably cumulative or duplicative, or can be obtained from some other source that is more convenient, less burdensome, or less expensive;

(ii) the party seeking discovery has had ample opportunity to obtain the information by discovery in the action; or

(iii) the burden or expense of the proposed discovery outweighs its likely benefit, considering the needs of the case, the amount in controversy, the parties' resources, the importance of the issues at stake in the action, and the importance of the discovery in resolving the issues.

(3) *Trial Preparation: Materials.*

(A) *Documents and Tangible Things.* Ordinarily, a party may not discover documents and tangible things that are prepared in anticipation of litigation or for trial by or for another party or its representative (including the other party's attorney, consultant, surety, indemnitor, insurer, or agent). But, subject to Rule 26(b)(4), those materials may be discovered if:

(i) they are otherwise discoverable under Rule 26(b)(1); and

(ii) the party shows that it has substantial need for the materials to prepare its case and cannot, without undue hardship, obtain their substantial equivalent by other means.

(B) *Protection Against Disclosure.* If the court orders discovery of those materials, it must protect against disclosure of the mental impressions, conclusions, opinions, or legal theories of a party's attorney or other representative concerning the litigation.

(C) *Previous Statement.* Any party or other person may, on request and without the required showing, obtain the person's own previous statement about the action or its subject matter. If the request is refused, the person may move for a court order, and Rule 37(a)(5)

applies to the award of expenses. A previous statement is either:

(i) a written statement that the person has signed or otherwise adopted or approved; or

(ii) a contemporaneous stenographic, mechanical, electrical, or other recording—or a transcription of it—that recites substantially verbatim the person's oral statement.

(4) *Trial Preparation: Experts.*

(A) *Deposition of an Expert Who May Testify.* A party may depose any person who has been identified as an expert whose opinions may be presented at trial. If Rule 26(a)(2)(B) requires a report from the expert, the deposition may be conducted only after the report is provided.

(B) *Trial–Preparation Protection for Draft Reports or Disclosures.* Rules 26(b)(3)(A) and (B) protect drafts of any report or disclosure required under Rule 26(a)(2), regardless of the form in which the draft is recorded.

(C) *Trial–Preparation Protection for Communications Between a Party's Attorney and Expert Witnesses.* Rules 26(b)(3)(A) and (B) protect communications between the party's attorney and any witness required to provide a report under Rule 26(a)(2)(B), regardless of the form of the communications, except to the extent that the communications:

(i) relate to compensation for the expert's study or testimony;

(ii) identify facts or data that the party's attorney provided and that the expert considered in forming the opinions to be expressed; or

(iii) identify assumptions that the party's attorney provided and that the expert relied on in forming the opinions to be expressed.

(D) *Expert Employed Only for Trial Preparation.* Ordinarily, a party may not, by interrogatories or deposition, discover facts known or opinions held by an expert who has been retained or specially employed by another party in anticipation of litigation or to prepare for trial and who is not expected to be called as a witness at trial. But a party may do so only:

  (i) as provided in Rule 35(b); or

  (ii) on showing exceptional circumstances under which it is impracticable for the party to obtain facts or opinions on the same subject by other means.

(E) *Payment.* Unless manifest injustice would result, the court must require that the party seeking discovery:

  (i) pay the expert a reasonable fee for time spent in responding to discovery under Rule 26(b)(4)(A) or (D); and

  (ii) for discovery under (D), also pay the other party a fair portion of the fees and expenses it reasonably incurred in obtaining the expert's facts and opinions.

(5) *Claiming Privilege or Protecting Trial-Preparation Materials.*

(A) *Information Withheld.* When a party withholds information otherwise discoverable by claiming that the information is privileged or subject to protection as trial-preparation material, the party must:

  (i) expressly make the claim; and

  (ii) describe the nature of the documents, communications, or tangible things not produced or disclosed—and do so in a manner that, without revealing information itself privileged or protected, will enable other parties to assess the claim.

(B) *Information Produced.* If information produced in discovery is subject to a claim of privilege or of protection as trial-preparation material, the party making the claim may notify any party that received the information of the claim and the basis for it. After being notified, a party must promptly return, sequester, or destroy the specified information and any copies it has; must not use or disclose the information until the claim is resolved; must take reasonable steps to retrieve the information if the party disclosed it before being notified; and may promptly present the information to the court under seal for a determination of the claim. The producing party must preserve the information until the claim is resolved.

[Text of subdivision (b) effective December 1, 2015, absent contrary Congressional action.]

(b) Discovery Scope and Limits.

(1) *Scope in General.* Unless otherwise limited by court order, the scope of discovery is as follows: Parties may obtain discovery regarding any non-privileged matter that is relevant to any party's claim or defense and proportional to the needs of the case, considering the importance of the issues at stake in the action, the amount in controversy, the parties' relative access to relevant information, the parties' resources, the importance of the discovery in resolving the issues, and whether the burden or expense of the proposed discovery outweighs its likely benefit. Information within this scope of discovery need not be admissible in evidence to be discoverable.

(2) *Limitations on Frequency and Extent.*

(A) *When Permitted.* By order, the court may alter the limits in these rules on the number of depositions and interrogatories or on the length of depositions under Rule 30. By order or local rule, the court may also limit the number of requests under Rule 36.

(B) *Specific Limitations on Electronically Stored Information.* A party need not provide discovery of electronically stored information from sources that the party identifies as not reasonably accessible because of undue burden or cost. On motion to compel discovery or for a protective order, the party from whom discovery is sought must show that the information is not reasonably accessible because of undue burden or cost. If that showing is made, the court may

14

nonetheless order discovery from such sources if the requesting party shows good cause, considering the limitations of Rule 26(b)(2)(C). The court may specify conditions for the discovery.

(C) *When Required.* On motion or on its own, the court must limit the frequency or extent of discovery otherwise allowed by these rules or by local rule if it determines that:

  (i) the discovery sought is unreasonably cumulative or duplicative, or can be obtained from some other source that is more convenient, less burdensome, or less expensive;

  (ii) the party seeking discovery has had ample opportunity to obtain the information by discovery in the action; or

  (iii) the proposed discovery is outside the scope permitted by Rule 26(b)(1).

(3) *Trial Preparation: Materials.*

(A) *Documents and Tangible Things.* Ordinarily, a party may not discover documents and tangible things that are prepared in anticipation of litigation or for trial by or for another party or its representative (including the other party's attorney, consultant, surety, indemnitor, insurer, or agent). But, subject to Rule 26(b)(4), those materials may be discovered if:

  (i) they are otherwise discoverable under Rule 26(b)(1); and

  (ii) the party shows that it has substantial need for the materials to prepare its case and cannot, without undue hardship, obtain their substantial equivalent by other means.

(B) *Protection Against Disclosure.* If the court orders discovery of those materials, it must protect against disclosure of the mental impressions, conclusions, opinions, or legal theories of a party's attorney or other representative concerning the litigation.

(C) *Previous Statement.* Any party or other person may, on request and without the required showing, obtain the person's own previous statement about the action or its subject matter. If the request is refused, the person may move for a court order, and Rule 37(a)(5) applies to the award of expenses. A previous statement is either:

  (i) a written statement that the person has signed or otherwise adopted or approved; or

  (ii) a contemporaneous stenographic, mechanical, electrical, or other recording—or a transcription of it—that recites substantially verbatim the person's oral statement.

(4) *Trial Preparation: Experts.*

(A) *Deposition of an Expert Who May Testify.* A party may depose any person who has been identified as an expert whose opinions may be presented at trial. If Rule 26(a)(2)(B) requires a report from the expert, the deposition may be conducted only after the report is provided.

(B) *Trial–Preparation Protection for Draft Reports or Disclosures.* Rules 26(b)(3)(A) and (B) protect drafts of any report or disclosure required under Rule 26(a)(2), regardless of the form in which the draft is recorded.

(C) *Trial–Preparation Protection for Communications Between a Party's Attorney and Expert Witnesses.* Rules 26(b)(3)(A) and (B) protect communications between the party's attorney and any witness required to provide a report under Rule 26(a)(2)(B), regardless of the form of the communications, except to the extent that the communications:

  (i) relate to compensation for the expert's study or testimony;

  (ii) identify facts or data that the party's attorney provided and that the expert considered in forming the opinions to be expressed; or

  (iii) identify assumptions that the party's attorney provided and that the expert relied on in forming the opinions to be expressed.

(D) *Expert Employed Only for Trial Preparation.* Ordinarily, a party may not, by interrogatories or deposition, discover facts known or opinions held by an expert who has been retained or specially employed by another party in anticipation of litigation or to prepare for trial and who is not expected to be called as a witness at trial. But a party may do so only:

    (i) as provided in Rule 35(b); or

    (ii) on showing exceptional circumstances under which it is impracticable for the party to obtain facts or opinions on the same subject by other means.

(E) *Payment.* Unless manifest injustice would result, the court must require that the party seeking discovery:

    (i) pay the expert a reasonable fee for time spent in responding to discovery under Rule 26(b)(4)(A) or (D); and

    (ii) for discovery under (D), also pay the other party a fair portion of the fees and expenses it reasonably incurred in obtaining the expert's facts and opinions.

(5) *Claiming Privilege or Protecting Trial-Preparation Materials.*

(A) *Information Withheld.* When a party withholds information otherwise discoverable by claiming that the information is privileged or subject to protection as trial-preparation material, the party must:

    (i) expressly make the claim; and

    (ii) describe the nature of the documents, communications, or tangible things not produced or disclosed—and do so in a manner that, without revealing information itself privileged or protected, will enable other parties to assess the claim.

(B) *Information Produced.* If information produced in discovery is subject to a claim of privilege or of protection as trial-preparation material, the party making the claim may notify any party that received the information of the claim and the basis for it. After being noti-fied, a party must promptly return, sequester, or destroy the specified information and any copies it has; must not use or disclose the information until the claim is resolved; must take reasonable steps to retrieve the information if the party disclosed it before being notified; and may promptly present the information to the court under seal for a determination of the claim. The producing party must preserve the information until the claim is resolved.

[Text of subdivision (c) effective until December 1, 2015, absent contrary Congressional action.]

(c) Protective Orders.

    (1) *In General.* A party or any person from whom discovery is sought may move for a protective order in the court where the action is pending—or as an alternative on matters relating to a deposition, in the court for the district where the deposition will be taken. The motion must include a certification that the movant has in good faith conferred or attempted to confer with other affected parties in an effort to resolve the dispute without court action. The court may, for good cause, issue an order to protect a party or person from annoyance, embarrassment, oppression, or undue burden or expense, including one or more of the following:

    (A) forbidding the disclosure or discovery;

    (B) specifying terms, including time and place, for the disclosure or discovery;

    (C) prescribing a discovery method other than the one selected by the party seeking discovery;

    (D) forbidding inquiry into certain matters, or limiting the scope of disclosure or discovery to certain matters;

    (E) designating the persons who may be present while the discovery is conducted;

    (F) requiring that a deposition be sealed and opened only on court order;

16

(G) requiring that a trade secret or other confidential research, development, or commercial information not be revealed or be revealed only in a specified way; and

(H) requiring that the parties simultaneously file specified documents or information in sealed envelopes, to be opened as the court directs.

(2) *Ordering Discovery.* If a motion for a protective order is wholly or partly denied, the court may, on just terms, order that any party or person provide or permit discovery.

(3) *Awarding Expenses.* Rule 37(a)(5) applies to the award of expenses.

[Text of subdivision (c) effective December 1, 2015, absent contrary Congressional action.]

(c) Protective Orders.

(1) *In General.* A party or any person from whom discovery is sought may move for a protective order in the court where the action is pending — or as an alternative on matters relating to a deposition, in the court for the district where the deposition will be taken. The motion must include a certification that the movant has in good faith conferred or attempted to confer with other affected parties in an effort to resolve the dispute without court action. The court may, for good cause, issue an order to protect a party or person from annoyance, embarrassment, oppression, or undue burden or expense, including one or more of the following:

(A) forbidding the disclosure or discovery;

(B) specifying terms, including time and place or the allocation of expenses, for the disclosure or discovery;

(C) prescribing a discovery method other than the one selected by the party seeking discovery;

(D) forbidding inquiry into certain matters, or limiting the scope of disclosure or discovery to certain matters;

(E) designating the persons who may be present while the discovery is conducted;

(F) requiring that a deposition be sealed and opened only on court order;

(G) requiring that a trade secret or other confidential research, development, or commercial information not be revealed or be revealed only in a specified way; and

(H) requiring that the parties simultaneously file specified documents or information in sealed envelopes, to be opened as the court directs.

(2) *Ordering Discovery.* If a motion for a protective order is wholly or partly denied, the court may, on just terms, order that any party or person provide or permit discovery.

(3) *Awarding Expenses.* Rule 37(a)(5) applies to the award of expenses.

[Text of subdivision (d) effective until December 1, 2015, absent contrary Congressional action.]

(d) Timing and Sequence of Discovery.

(1) *Timing.* A party may not seek discovery from any source before the parties have conferred as required by Rule 26(f), except in a proceeding exempted from initial disclosure under Rule 26(a)(1)(B), or when authorized by these rules, by stipulation, or by court order.

(2) *Sequence.* Unless, on motion, the court orders otherwise for the parties' and witnesses' convenience and in the interests of justice:

(A) methods of discovery may be used in any sequence; and

(B) discovery by one party does not require any other party to delay its discovery.

[Text of subdivision (d) effective December 1, 2015, absent contrary Congressional action.]

(d) Timing and Sequence of Discovery.

(1) *Timing.* A party may not seek discovery from any source before the parties have conferred as required by Rule 26(f), except in a proceeding exempted from initial disclosure under Rule 26(a)(1)(B), or when authorized by these rules, by stipulation, or by court order.

(2) Early Rule 34 Requests.

    (A) *Time to Deliver.* More than 21 days after the summons and complaint are served on a party, a request under Rule 34 may be delivered:

        (i) to that party by any other party, and

        (ii) by that party to any plaintiff or to any other party that has been served.

    (B) *When Considered Served.* The request is considered to have been served at the first Rule 26(f) conference.

(3) Sequence. Unless the parties stipulate or the court orders otherwise for the parties' and witnesses' convenience and in the interests of justice:

    (A) methods of discovery may be used in any sequence; and

    (B) discovery by one party does not require any other party to delay its discovery.

(e) Supplementing Disclosures and Responses.

(1) In General. A party who has made a disclosure under Rule 26(a)—or who has responded to an interrogatory, request for production, or request for admission—must supplement or correct its disclosure or response:

    (A) in a timely manner if the party learns that in some material respect the disclosure or response is incomplete or incorrect, and if the additional or corrective information has not otherwise been made known to the other parties during the discovery process or in writing; or

    (B) as ordered by the court.

(2) Expert Witness. For an expert whose report must be disclosed under Rule 26(a)(2)(B), the party's duty to supplement extends both to information included in the report and to information given during the expert's deposition. Any additions or changes to this information must be disclosed by the time the party's pretrial disclosures under Rule 26(a)(3) are due.

[Text of subdivision (f) effective until December 1, 2015, absent contrary Congressional action.]

(f) Conference of the Parties; Planning for Discovery.

(1) Conference Timing. Except in a proceeding exempted from initial disclosure under Rule 26(a)(1)(B) or when the court orders otherwise, the parties must confer as soon as practicable—and in any event at least 21 days before a scheduling conference is to be held or a scheduling order is due under Rule 16(b).

(2) Conference Content; Parties' Responsibilities. In conferring, the parties must consider the nature and basis of their claims and defenses and the possibilities for promptly settling or resolving the case; make or arrange for the disclosures required by Rule 26(a)(1); discuss any issues about preserving discoverable information; and develop a proposed discovery plan. The attorneys of record and all unrepresented parties that have appeared in the case are jointly responsible for arranging the conference, for attempting in good faith to agree on the proposed discovery plan, and for submitting to the court within 14 days after the conference a written report outlining the plan. The court may order the parties or attorneys to attend the conference in person.

(3) Discovery Plan. A discovery plan must state the parties' views and proposals on:

    (A) what changes should be made in the timing, form, or requirement for disclosures under Rule 26(a), including a statement of when initial disclosures were made or will be made;

    (B) the subjects on which discovery may be needed, when discovery should be completed, and whether discovery should be conducted in phases or be limited to or focused on particular issues;

    (C) any issues about disclosure or discovery of electronically stored information, including the form or forms in which it should be produced;

(D) any issues about claims of privilege or of protection as trial-preparation materials, including—if the parties agree on a procedure to assert these claims after production—whether to ask the court to include their agreement in an order;

(E) what changes should be made in the limitations on discovery imposed under these rules or by local rule, and what other limitations should be imposed; and

(F) any other orders that the court should issue under Rule 26(c) or under Rule 16(b) and (c).

(4) *Expedited Schedule.* If necessary to comply with its expedited schedule for Rule 16(b) conferences, a court may by local rule:

(A) require the parties' conference to occur less than 21 days before the scheduling conference is held or a scheduling order is due under Rule 16(b); and

(B) require the written report outlining the discovery plan to be filed less than 14 days after the parties' conference, or excuse the parties from submitting a written report and permit them to report orally on their discovery plan at the Rule 16(b) conference.

[Text of subdivision (f) effective December 1, 2015, absent contrary Congressional action.]

(f) Conference of the Parties; Planning for Discovery.

(1) *Conference Timing.* Except in a proceeding exempted from initial disclosure under Rule 26(a)(1)(B) or when the court orders otherwise, the parties must confer as soon as practicable—and in any event at least 21 days before a scheduling conference is to be held or a scheduling order is due under Rule 16(b).

(2) *Conference Content; Parties' Responsibilities.* In conferring, the parties must consider the nature and basis of their claims and defenses and the possibilities for promptly settling or resolving the case; make or arrange for the disclosures required by Rule 26(a)(1); discuss any issues about preserving discoverable information; and develop a proposed discovery plan. The attorneys of record and all unrepresented parties that have appeared in the case are jointly responsible for arranging the conference, for attempting in good faith to agree on the proposed discovery plan, and for submitting to the court within 14 days after the conference a written report outlining the plan. The court may order the parties or attorneys to attend the conference in person.

(3) *Discovery Plan.* A discovery plan must state the parties' views and proposals on:

(A) what changes should be made in the timing, form, or requirement for disclosures under Rule 26(a), including a statement of when initial disclosures were made or will be made;

(B) the subjects on which discovery may be needed, when discovery should be completed, and whether discovery should be conducted in phases or be limited to or focused on particular issues;

(C) any issues about disclosure, discovery, or preservation of electronically stored information, including the form or forms in which it should be produced;

(D) any issues about claims of privilege or of protection as trial-preparation materials, including — if the parties agree on a procedure to assert these claims after production — whether to ask the court to include their agreement in an order under Federal Rule of Evidence 502;

(E) what changes should be made in the limitations on discovery imposed under these rules or by local rule, and what other limitations should be imposed; and

(F) any other orders that the court should issue under Rule 26(c) or under Rule 16(b) and (c).

(4) *Expedited Schedule.* If necessary to comply with its expedited schedule for Rule 16(b) conferences, a court may by local rule:

(A) require the parties' conference to occur less than 21 days before the scheduling conference is held or a scheduling order is due under Rule 16(b); and

(B) require the written report outlining the discovery plan to be filed less than 14 days after the parties' conference, or excuse the parties from submitting a written report and permit them to report orally on their discovery plan at the Rule 16(b) conference.

(g) Signing Disclosures and Discovery Requests, Responses, and Objections.

(1) *Signature Required; Effect of Signature.* Every disclosure under Rule 26(a)(1) or (a)(3) and every discovery request, response, or objection must be signed by at least one attorney of record in the attorney's own name— or by the party personally, if unrepresented—and must state the signer's address, e-mail address, and telephone number. By signing, an attorney or party certifies that to the best of the person's knowledge, information, and belief formed after a reasonable inquiry:

(A) with respect to a disclosure, it is complete and correct as of the time it is made; and

(B) with respect to a discovery request, response, or objection, it is:

(i) consistent with these rules and warranted by existing law or by a nonfrivolous argument for extending, modifying, or reversing existing law, or for establishing new law;

(ii) not interposed for any improper purpose, such as to harass, cause unnecessary delay, or needlessly increase the cost of litigation; and

(iii) neither unreasonable nor unduly burdensome or expensive, considering the needs of the case, prior discovery in the case, the amount in controversy, and the importance of the issues at stake in the action.

(2) *Failure to Sign.* Other parties have no duty to act on an unsigned disclosure, request, response, or objection until it is signed, and the court must strike it unless a signature is promptly supplied after the omission is called to the attorney's or party's attention.

(3) *Sanction for Improper Certification.* If a certification violates this rule without substantial justification, the court, on motion or on its own, must impose an appropriate sanction on the signer, the party on whose behalf the signer was acting, or both. The sanction may include an order to pay the reasonable expenses, including attorney's fees, caused by the violation.

(Amended December 27, 1946, effective March 19, 1948; January 21, 1963, effective July 1, 1963; February 28, 1966, effective July 1, 1966; March 30, 1970, effective July 1, 1970; April 29, 1980, effective August 1, 1980; April 28, 1983, effective August 1, 1983; March 2, 1987, effective August 1, 1987; April 22, 1993, effective December 1, 1993; April 17, 2000, effective December 1, 2000; April 12, 2006, effective December 1, 2006; April 30, 2007, effective December 1, 2007; April 28, 2010, effective December 1, 2010; April 29, 2015, effective December 1, 2015, absent contrary Congressional action.)

RULE 30. DEPOSITIONS BY ORAL EXAMINATION

[Text of subdivision (a) effective until December 1, 2015, absent contrary Congressional action.]

(a) When a Deposition May Be Taken.

(1) *Without Leave.* A party may, by oral questions, depose any person, including a party, without leave of court except as provided in Rule 30(a)(2). The deponent's attendance may be compelled by subpoena under Rule 45.

(2) *With Leave.* A party must obtain leave of court, and the court must grant leave to the extent consistent with Rule 26(b)(2):

(A) if the parties have not stipulated to the deposition and:

(i) the deposition would result in more than 10 depositions being taken under this rule or Rule 31 by the plaintiffs, or by the defendants, or by the third-party defendants;

(ii) the deponent has already been deposed in the case; or

      (iii) the party seeks to take the deposition before the time specified in Rule 26(d), unless the party certifies in the notice, with supporting facts, that the deponent is expected to leave the United States and be unavailable for examination in this country after that time; or

   (B) if the deponent is confined in prison.

[Text of subdivision (a) effective December 1, 2015, absent contrary Congressional action.]

(a) When a Deposition May Be Taken.

   (1) *Without Leave.* A party may, by oral questions, depose any person, including a party, without leave of court except as provided in Rule 30(a)(2). The deponent's attendance may be compelled by subpoena under Rule 45.

   (2) *With Leave.* A party must obtain leave of court, and the court must grant leave to the extent consistent with Rule 26(b)(1) and (2):

   (A) if the parties have not stipulated to the deposition and:

      (i) the deposition would result in more than 10 depositions being taken under this rule or Rule 31 by the plaintiffs, or by the defendants, or by the third-party defendants;

      (ii) the deponent has already been deposed in the case; or

      (iii) the party seeks to take the deposition before the time specified in Rule 26(d), unless the party certifies in the notice, with supporting facts, that the deponent is expected to leave the United States and be unavailable for examination in this country after that time; or

   (B) if the deponent is confined in prison.

(b) Notice of the Deposition; Other Formal Requirements.

   (1) *Notice in General.* A party who wants to depose a person by oral questions must give reasonable written notice to every other party. The notice must state the time and place of the deposition and, if known, the deponent's name and address. If the name is unknown, the notice must provide a general description sufficient to identify the person or the particular class or group to which the person belongs.

   (2) *Producing Documents.* If a subpoena duces tecum is to be served on the deponent, the materials designated for production, as set out in the subpoena, must be listed in the notice or in an attachment. The notice to a party deponent may be accompanied by a request under Rule 34 to produce documents and tangible things at the deposition.

   (3) *Method of Recording.*

   (A) *Method Stated in the Notice.* The party who notices the deposition must state in the notice the method for recording the testimony. Unless the court orders otherwise, testimony may be recorded by audio, audiovisual, or stenographic means. The noticing party bears the recording costs. Any party may arrange to transcribe a deposition.

   (B) *Additional Method.* With prior notice to the deponent and other parties, any party may designate another method for recording the testimony in addition to that specified in the original notice. That party bears the expense of the additional record or transcript unless the court orders otherwise.

   (4) *By Remote Means.* The parties may stipulate—or the court may on motion order—that a deposition be taken by telephone or other remote means. For the purpose of this rule and Rules 28(a), 37(a)(2), and 37(b)(1), the deposition takes place where the deponent answers the questions.

   (5) *Officer's Duties.*

   (A) *Before the Deposition.* Unless the parties stipulate otherwise, a deposition must be conducted before an officer appointed or designated under Rule 28. The officer must begin the deposition with an on-the-record statement that includes:

(i) the officer's name and business address;

(ii) the date, time, and place of the deposition;

(iii) the deponent's name;

(iv) the officer's administration of the oath or affirmation to the deponent; and

(v) the identity of all persons present.

(B) *Conducting the Deposition; Avoiding Distortion.* If the deposition is recorded non-stenographically, the officer must repeat the items in Rule 30(b)(5)(A)(i)-(iii) at the beginning of each unit of the recording medium. The deponent's and attorneys' appearance or demeanor must not be distorted through recording techniques.

(C) *After the Deposition.* At the end of a deposition, the officer must state on the record that the deposition is complete and must set out any stipulations made by the attorneys about custody of the transcript or recording and of the exhibits, or about any other pertinent matters.

(6) *Notice or Subpoena Directed to an Organization.* In its notice or subpoena, a party may name as the deponent a public or private corporation, a partnership, an association, a governmental agency, or other entity and must describe with reasonable particularity the matters for examination. The named organization must then designate one or more officers, directors, or managing agents, or designate other persons who consent to testify on its behalf; and it may set out the matters on which each person designated will testify. A subpoena must advise a nonparty organization of its duty to make this designation. The persons designated must testify about information known or reasonably available to the organization. This paragraph (6) does not preclude a deposition by any other procedure allowed by these rules.

(c) **Examination and Cross–Examination; Record of the Examination; Objections; Written Questions.**

(1) *Examination and Cross–Examination.* The examination and cross-examination of a deponent proceed as they would at trial under the Federal Rules of Evidence, except Rules 103 and 615. After putting the deponent under oath or affirmation, the officer must record the testimony by the method designated under Rule 30(b)(3)(A). The testimony must be recorded by the officer personally or by a person acting in the presence and under the direction of the officer.

(2) *Objections.* An objection at the time of the examination—whether to evidence, to a party's conduct, to the officer's qualifications, to the manner of taking the deposition, or to any other aspect of the deposition—must be noted on the record, but the examination still proceeds; the testimony is taken subject to any objection. An objection must be stated concisely in a nonargumentative and nonsuggestive manner. A person may instruct a deponent not to answer only when necessary to preserve a privilege, to enforce a limitation ordered by the court, or to present a motion under Rule 30(d)(3).

(3) *Participating Through Written Questions.* Instead of participating in the oral examination, a party may serve written questions in a sealed envelope on the party noticing the deposition, who must deliver them to the officer. The officer must ask the deponent those questions and record the answers verbatim.

[Text of subdivision (d) effective until December 1, 2015, absent contrary Congressional action.]

(d) **Duration; Sanction; Motion to Terminate or Limit.**

(1) *Duration.* Unless otherwise stipulated or ordered by the court, a deposition is limited to 1 day of 7 hours. The court must allow additional time consistent with Rule 26(b)(2) if needed to fairly examine the deponent or if the deponent, another person, or any other circumstance impedes or delays the examination.

(2) *Sanction.* The court may impose an appropriate sanction—including the reasonable expenses and attorney's fees incurred by any party—on a person who impedes, delays, or frus-

trates the fair examination of the deponent.

(3) *Motion to Terminate or Limit.*

(A) *Grounds.* At any time during a deposition, the deponent or a party may move to terminate or limit it on the ground that it is being conducted in bad faith or in a manner that unreasonably annoys, embarrasses, or oppresses the deponent or party. The motion may be filed in the court where the action is pending or the deposition is being taken. If the objecting deponent or party so demands, the deposition must be suspended for the time necessary to obtain an order.

(B) *Order.* The court may order that the deposition be terminated or may limit its scope and manner as provided in Rule 26(c). If terminated, the deposition may be resumed only by order of the court where the action is pending.

(C) *Award of Expenses.* Rule 37(a)(5) applies to the award of expenses.

[Text of subdivision (d) effective December 1, 2015, absent contrary Congressional action.]

(d) Duration; Sanction; Motion to Terminate or Limit.

(1) *Duration.* Unless otherwise stipulated or ordered by the court, a deposition is limited to one day of 7 hours. The court must allow additional time consistent with Rule 26(b)(1) and (2) if needed to fairly examine the deponent or if the deponent, another person, or any other circumstance impedes or delays the examination.

(2) *Sanction.* The court may impose an appropriate sanction—including the reasonable expenses and attorney's fees incurred by any party—on a person who impedes, delays, or frustrates the fair examination of the deponent.

(3) *Motion to Terminate or Limit.*

(A) *Grounds.* At any time during a deposition, the deponent or a party may move to terminate or limit it on the ground that it is being conducted in bad faith or in a manner that unreasonably annoys, embarrasses, or oppresses the depo-

nent or party. The motion may be filed in the court where the action is pending or the deposition is being taken. If the objecting deponent or party so demands, the deposition must be suspended for the time necessary to obtain an order.

(B) *Order.* The court may order that the deposition be terminated or may limit its scope and manner as provided in Rule 26(c). If terminated, the deposition may be resumed only by order of the court where the action is pending.

(C) *Award of Expenses.* Rule 37(a)(5) applies to the award of expenses.

(e) Review by the Witness; Changes.

(1) *Review; Statement of Changes.* On request by the deponent or a party before the deposition is completed, the deponent must be allowed 30 days after being notified by the officer that the transcript or recording is available in which:

(A) to review the transcript or recording; and

(B) if there are changes in form or substance, to sign a statement listing the changes and the reasons for making them.

(2) *Changes Indicated in the Officer's Certificate.* The officer must note in the certificate prescribed by Rule 30(f)(1) whether a review was requested and, if so, must attach any changes the deponent makes during the 30–day period.

(f) Certification and Delivery; Exhibits; Copies of the Transcript or Recording; Filing.

(1) *Certification and Delivery.* The officer must certify in writing that the witness was duly sworn and that the deposition accurately records the witness's testimony. The certificate must accompany the record of the deposition. Unless the court orders otherwise, the officer must seal the deposition in an envelope or package bearing the title of the action and marked "Deposition of [witness's name]" and must promptly send it to the attorney who arranged for the transcript or recording. The attorney must store it under conditions that will protect it against loss, destruction, tampering, or deterioration. ·

(2) Documents and Tangible Things.

  (A) *Originals and Copies.* Documents and tangible things produced for inspection during a deposition must, on a party's request, be marked for identification and attached to the deposition. Any party may inspect and copy them. But if the person who produced them wants to keep the originals, the person may:

    (i) offer copies to be marked, attached to the deposition, and then used as originals—after giving all parties a fair opportunity to verify the copies by comparing them with the originals; or

    (ii) give all parties a fair opportunity to inspect and copy the originals after they are marked—in which event the originals may be used as if attached to the deposition.

  (B) *Order Regarding the Originals.* Any party may move for an order that the originals be attached to the deposition pending final disposition of the case.

(3) *Copies of the Transcript or Recording.* Unless otherwise stipulated or ordered by the court, the officer must retain the stenographic notes of a deposition taken stenographically or a copy of the recording of a deposition taken by another method. When paid reasonable charges, the officer must furnish a copy of the transcript or recording to any party or the deponent.

(4) *Notice of Filing.* A party who files the deposition must promptly notify all other parties of the filing.

(g) Failure to Attend a Deposition or Serve a Subpoena; Expenses. A party who, expecting a deposition to be taken, attends in person or by an attorney may recover reasonable expenses for attending, including attorney's fees, if the noticing party failed to:

(1) attend and proceed with the deposition; or

(2) serve a subpoena on a nonparty deponent, who consequently did not attend.

(Amended January 21, 1963, effective July 1, 1963; March 30, 1970, effective July 1, 1970; March 1, 1971, effective July 1, 1971; November 20, 1972, effective July 1, 1975; April 29, 1980, effective August 1, 1980; March 2, 1987, effective August 1, 1987; April 22, 1993, effective December 1, 1993; April 17, 2000, effective December 1, 2000; April 30, 2007, effective December 1, 2007; April 29, 2015, effective December 1, 2015, absent contrary Congressional action.)

RULE 31. DEPOSITIONS BY WRITTEN QUESTIONS

[Text of subdivision (a) effective until December 1, 2015, absent contrary Congressional action.]

(a) When a Deposition May Be Taken.

(1) *Without Leave.* A party may, by written questions, depose any person, including a party, without leave of court except as provided in Rule 31(a)(2). The deponent's attendance may be compelled by subpoena under Rule 45.

(2) *With Leave.* A party must obtain leave of court, and the court must grant leave to the extent consistent with Rule 26(b)(2):

  (A) if the parties have not stipulated to the deposition and:

    (i) the deposition would result in more than 10 depositions being taken under this rule or Rule 30 by the plaintiffs, or by the defendants, or by the third-party defendants;

    (ii) the deponent has already been deposed in the case; or

    (iii) the party seeks to take a deposition before the time specified in Rule 26(d); or

  (B) if the deponent is confined in prison.

(3) *Service; Required Notice.* A party who wants to depose a person by written questions must serve them on every other party, with a notice stating, if known, the deponent's name and address. If the name is unknown, the notice must provide a general description sufficient to identify the person or the particular class or group to which the person belongs. The notice must also state the name or descriptive title and the address of the officer before whom the deposition will be taken.

(4) *Questions Directed to an Organization.* A public or private corporation, a partnership, an association, or a governmental agency may be deposed by written questions in accordance with Rule 30(b)(6).

(5) *Questions from Other Parties.* Any questions to the deponent from other parties must be served on all parties as follows: cross-questions, within 14 days after being served with the notice and direct questions; redirect questions, within 7 days after being served with cross-questions; and re-cross-questions, within 7 days after being served with redirect questions. The court may, for good cause, extend or shorten these times.

[Text of subdivision (a) effective December 1, 2015, absent contrary Congressional action.]

(a) **When a Deposition May Be Taken.**

(1) *Without Leave.* A party may, by written questions, depose any person, including a party, without leave of court except as provided in Rule 31(a)(2). The deponent's attendance may be compelled by subpoena under Rule 45.

(2) *With Leave.* A party must obtain leave of court, and the court must grant leave to the extent consistent with Rule 26(b)(1) and (2):

(A) if the parties have not stipulated to the deposition and:

(i) the deposition would result in more than 10 depositions being taken under this rule or Rule 30 by the plaintiffs, or by the defendants, or by the third-party defendants;

(ii) the deponent has already been deposed in the case; or

(iii) the party seeks to take a deposition before the time specified in Rule 26(d); or

(B) if the deponent is confined in prison.

(3) *Service; Required Notice.* A party who wants to depose a person by written questions must serve them on every other party, with a notice stating, if known, the deponent's name and address. If the name is unknown, the notice must provide a general description sufficient to identify the person or the particular class or group to which the person belongs. The notice must also state the name or descriptive title and the address of the officer before whom the deposition will be taken.

(4) *Questions Directed to an Organization.* A public or private corporation, a partnership, an association, or a governmental agency may be deposed by written questions in accordance with Rule 30(b)(6).

(5) *Questions from Other Parties.* Any questions to the deponent from other parties must be served on all parties as follows: cross-questions, within 14 days after being served with the notice and direct questions; redirect questions, within 7 days after being served with cross-questions; and re-cross-questions, within 7 days after being served with redirect questions. The court may, for good cause, extend or shorten these times.

(b) **Delivery to the Officer; Officer's Duties.** The party who noticed the deposition must deliver to the officer a copy of all the questions served and of the notice. The officer must promptly proceed in the manner provided in Rule 30(c), (e), and (f) to:

(1) take the deponent's testimony in response to the questions;

(2) prepare and certify the deposition; and

(3) send it to the party, attaching a copy of the questions and of the notice.

(c) **Notice of Completion or Filing.**

(1) *Completion.* The party who noticed the deposition must notify all other parties when it is completed.

(2) *Filing.* A party who files the deposition must promptly notify all other parties of the filing.

(Amended March 30, 1970, effective July 1, 1970; March 2, 1987, effective August 1, 1987; April 22, 1993, effective December 1, 1993; April 30, 2007, effective December 1, 2007; April 29, 2015, effective December 1, 2015, absent contrary Congressional action.)

RULE 33. INTERROGATORIES TO PARTIES

[Text of subdivision (a) effective until December 1, 2015, absent contrary Congressional action.]

(a) In General.

(1) **Number.** Unless otherwise stipulated or ordered by the court, a party may serve on any other party no more than 25 written interrogatories, including all discrete subparts. Leave to serve additional interrogatories may be granted to the extent consistent with Rule 26(b)(2).

(2) **Scope.** An interrogatory may relate to any matter that may be inquired into under Rule 26(b). An interrogatory is not objectionable merely because it asks for an opinion or contention that relates to fact or the application of law to fact, but the court may order that the interrogatory need not be answered until designated discovery is complete, or until a pretrial conference or some other time.

[Text of subdivision (a) effective December 1, 2015, absent contrary Congressional action.]

(a) In General.

(1) **Number.** Unless otherwise stipulated or ordered by the court, a party may serve on any other party no more than 25 written interrogatories, including all discrete subparts. Leave to serve additional interrogatories may be granted to the extent consistent with Rule 26(b)(1) and (2).

(2) **Scope.** An interrogatory may relate to any matter that may be inquired into under Rule 26(b). An interrogatory is not objectionable merely because it asks for an opinion or contention that relates to fact or the application of law to fact, but the court may order that the interrogatory need not be answered until designated discovery is complete, or until a pretrial conference or some other time.

(b) Answers and Objections.

(1) **Responding Party.** The interrogatories must be answered:

(A) by the party to whom they are directed; or

(B) if that party is a public or private corporation, a partnership, an association, or a governmental agency, by any officer or agent, who must furnish the information available to the party.

(2) **Time to Respond.** The responding party must serve its answers and any objections within 30 days after being served with the interrogatories. A shorter or longer time may be stipulated to under Rule 29 or be ordered by the court.

(3) **Answering Each Interrogatory.** Each interrogatory must, to the extent it is not objected to, be answered separately and fully in writing under oath.

(4) **Objections.** The grounds for objecting to an interrogatory must be stated with specificity. Any ground not stated in a timely objection is waived unless the court, for good cause, excuses the failure.

(5) **Signature.** The person who makes the answers must sign them, and the attorney who objects must sign any objections.

(c) Use.
An answer to an interrogatory may be used to the extent allowed by the Federal Rules of Evidence.

(d) Option to Produce Business Records.
If the answer to an interrogatory may be determined by examining, auditing, compiling, abstracting, or summarizing a party's business records (including electronically stored information), and if the burden of deriving or ascertaining the answer will be substantially the same for either party, the responding party may answer by:

(1) specifying the records that must be reviewed, in sufficient detail to enable the interrogating party to locate and identify them as readily as the responding party could; and

(2) giving the interrogating party a reasonable opportunity to examine and audit the records and to make copies,

compilations, abstracts, or summaries.

(Amended December 27, 1946, effective March 19, 1948; March 30, 1970, effective July 1, 1970; April 29, 1980, effective August 1, 1980; April 22, 1993, effective December 1, 1993; April 12, 2006, effective December 1, 2006; April 30, 2007, effective December 1, 2007; April 29, 2015, effective December 1, 2015, absent contrary Congressional action.)

RULE 34. PRODUCING DOCUMENTS, ELECTRONICALLY STORED INFORMATION, AND TANGIBLE THINGS, OR ENTERING ONTO LAND, FOR INSPECTION AND OTHER PURPOSES

(a) **In General.** A party may serve on any other party a request within the scope of Rule 26(b):

(1) to produce and permit the requesting party or its representative to inspect, copy, test, or sample the following items in the responding party's possession, custody, or control:

(A) any designated documents or electronically stored information—including writings, drawings, graphs, charts, photographs, sound recordings, images, and other data or data compilations—stored in any medium from which information can be obtained either directly or, if necessary, after translation by the responding party into a reasonably usable form; or

(B) any designated tangible things; or

(2) to permit entry onto designated land or other property possessed or controlled by the responding party, so that the requesting party may inspect, measure, survey, photograph, test, or sample the property or any designated object or operation on it.

[Text of subdivision (b) effective until December 1, 2015, absent contrary Congressional action.]

(b) **Procedure.**

(1) ***Contents of the Request.*** The request:

(A) must describe with reasonable particularity each item or category of items to be inspected;

(B) must specify a reasonable time, place, and manner for the inspection and for performing the related acts; and

(C) may specify the form or forms in which electronically stored information is to be produced.

(2) ***Responses and Objections.***

(A) *Time to Respond.* The party to whom the request is directed must respond in writing within 30 days after being served. A shorter or longer time may be stipulated to under Rule 29 or be ordered by the court.

(B) *Responding to Each Item.* For each item or category, the response must either state that inspection and related activities will be permitted as requested or state an objection to the request, including the reasons.

(C) *Objections.* An objection to part of a request must specify the part and permit inspection of the rest.

(D) *Responding to a Request for Production of Electronically Stored Information.* The response may state an objection to a requested form for producing electronically stored information. If the responding party objects to a requested form—or if no form was specified in the request—the party must state the form or forms it intends to use.

(E) *Producing the Documents or Electronically Stored Information.* Unless otherwise stipulated or ordered by the court, these procedures apply to producing documents or electronically stored information:

(i) A party must produce documents as they are kept in the usual course of business or must organize and label them to correspond to the categories in the request;

(ii) If a request does not specify a form for producing electronically stored information, a party must produce it in a form or forms in which it is ordinarily maintained or in a reasonably usable form or forms; and

27

(iii) A party need not produce the same electronically stored information in more than one form.

[Text of subdivision (b) effective December 1, 2015, absent contrary Congressional action.]

(b) Procedure.

(1) **Contents of the Request.** The request:

(A) must describe with reasonable particularity each item or category of items to be inspected;

(B) must specify a reasonable time, place, and manner for the inspection and for performing the related acts; and

(C) may specify the form or forms in which electronically stored information is to be produced.

(2) **Responses and Objections.**

(A) *Time to Respond.* The party to whom the request is directed must respond in writing within 30 days after being served or — if the request was delivered under Rule 26(d)(2) — within 30 days after the parties' first Rule 26(f) conference. A shorter or longer time may be stipulated to under Rule 29 or be ordered by the court.

(B) *Responding to Each Item.* For each item or category, the response must either state that inspection and related activities will be permitted as requested or state with specificity the grounds for objecting to the request, including the reasons. The responding party may state that it will produce copies of documents or of electronically stored information instead of permitting inspection. The production must then be completed no later than the time for inspection specified in the request or another reasonable time specified in the response.

(C) *Objections.* An objection must state whether any responsive materials are being withheld on the basis of that objection. An objection to part of a request must specify the part and permit inspection of the rest.

(D) *Responding to a Request for Production of Electronically Stored*

Information. The response may state an objection to a requested form for producing electronically stored information. If the responding party objects to a requested form—or if no form was specified in the request—the party must state the form or forms it intends to use.

(E) *Producing the Documents or Electronically Stored Information.* Unless otherwise stipulated or ordered by the court, these procedures apply to producing documents or electronically stored information:

(i) A party must produce documents as they are kept in the usual course of business or must organize and label them to correspond to the categories in the request;

(ii) If a request does not specify a form for producing electronically stored information, a party must produce it in a form or forms in which it is ordinarily maintained or in a reasonably usable form or forms; and

(iii) A party need not produce the same electronically stored information in more than one form.

(c) Nonparties. As provided in Rule 45, a nonparty may be compelled to produce documents and tangible things or to permit an inspection.

(Amended December 27, 1946, effective March 19, 1948; March 30, 1970, effective July 1, 1970; April 29, 1980, effective August 1, 1980; March 2, 1987, effective August 1, 1987; April 30, 1991, effective December 1, 1991; April 22, 1993, effective December 1, 1993; April 12, 2006, effective December 1, 2006; April 30, 2007, effective December 1, 2007; April 29, 2015, effective December 1, 2015, absent contrary Congressional action.)

RULE 37. FAILURE TO MAKE DISCLOSURES OR TO COOPERATE IN DISCOVERY; SANCTIONS

[Text of subdivision (a) effective until December 1, 2015, absent contrary Congressional action.]

(a) Motion for an Order Compelling Disclosure or Discovery.

(1) *In General.* On notice to other parties and all affected persons, a party may move for an order compelling disclosure or discovery. The motion must include a certification that the movant has in good faith conferred or attempted to confer with the person or party failing to make disclosure or discovery in an effort to obtain it without court action.

(2) *Appropriate Court.* A motion for an order to a party must be made in the court where the action is pending. A motion for an order to a nonparty must be made in the court where the discovery is or will be taken.

(3) *Specific Motions.*

(A) *To Compel Disclosure.* If a party fails to make a disclosure required by Rule 26(a), any other party may move to compel disclosure and for appropriate sanctions.

(B) *To Compel a Discovery Response.* A party seeking discovery may move for an order compelling an answer, designation, production, or inspection. This motion may be made if:

(i) a deponent fails to answer a question asked under Rule 30 or 31;

(ii) a corporation or other entity fails to make a designation under Rule 30(b)(6) or 31(a)(4);

(iii) a party fails to answer an interrogatory submitted under Rule 33; or

(iv) a party fails to respond that inspection will be permitted—or fails to permit inspection—as requested under Rule 34.

(C) *Related to a Deposition.* When taking an oral deposition, the party asking a question may complete or adjourn the examination before moving for an order.

(4) *Evasive or Incomplete Disclosure, Answer, or Response.* For purposes of this subdivision (a), an evasive or incomplete disclosure, answer, or response must be treated as a failure to disclose, answer, or respond.

(5) *Payment of Expenses; Protective Orders.*

(A) *If the Motion Is Granted (or Disclosure or Discovery Is Provided After Filing).* If the motion is granted—or if the disclosure or requested discovery is provided after the motion was filed—the court must, after giving an opportunity to be heard, require the party or deponent whose conduct necessitated the motion, the party or attorney advising that conduct, or both to pay the movant's reasonable expenses incurred in making the motion, including attorney's fees. But the court must not order this payment if:

(i) the movant filed the motion before attempting in good faith to obtain the disclosure or discovery without court action;

(ii) the opposing party's nondisclosure, response, or objection was substantially justified; or

(iii) other circumstances make an award of expenses unjust.

(B) *If the Motion Is Denied.* If the motion is denied, the court may issue any protective order authorized under Rule 26(c) and must, after giving an opportunity to be heard, require the movant, the attorney filing the motion, or both to pay the party or deponent who opposed the motion its reasonable expenses incurred in opposing the motion, including attorney's fees. But the court must not order this payment if the motion was substantially justified or other circumstances make an award of expenses unjust.

(C) *If the Motion Is Granted in Part and Denied in Part.* If the motion is granted in part and denied in part, the court may issue any protective order authorized under Rule 26(c) and may, after giving an opportunity to be heard, apportion the reasonable expenses for the motion.

[Text of subdivision (a) effective December 1, 2015, absent contrary Congressional action.]

(a) **Motion for an Order Compelling Disclosure or Discovery.**

(1) *In General.* On notice to other parties and all affected persons, a party

may move for an order compelling disclosure or discovery. The motion must include a certification that the movant has in good faith conferred or attempted to confer with the person or party failing to make disclosure or discovery in an effort to obtain it without court action.

(2) *Appropriate Court.* A motion for an order to a party must be made in the court where the action is pending. A motion for an order to a nonparty must be made in the court where the discovery is or will be taken.

(3) *Specific Motions.*

 (A) *To Compel Disclosure.* If a party fails to make a disclosure required by Rule 26(a), any other party may move to compel disclosure and for appropriate sanctions.

 (B) *To Compel a Discovery Response.* A party seeking discovery may move for an order compelling an answer, designation, production, or inspection. This motion may be made if:

  (i) a deponent fails to answer a question asked under Rule 30 or 31;

  (ii) a corporation or other entity fails to make a designation under Rule 30(b)(6) or 31(a)(4);

  (iii) a party fails to answer an interrogatory submitted under Rule 33; or

  (iv) a party fails to produce documents or fails to respond that inspection will be permitted — or fails to permit inspection — as requested under Rule 34.

 (C) *Related to a Deposition.* When taking an oral deposition, the party asking a question may complete or adjourn the examination before moving for an order.

(4) *Evasive or Incomplete Disclosure, Answer, or Response.* For purposes of this subdivision (a), an evasive or incomplete disclosure, answer, or response must be treated as a failure to disclose, answer, or respond.

(5) *Payment of Expenses; Protective Orders.*

 (A) *If the Motion Is Granted (or Disclosure or Discovery Is Provided After Filing).* If the motion is granted—or if the disclosure or requested discovery is provided after the motion was filed—the court must, after giving an opportunity to be heard, require the party or deponent whose conduct necessitated the motion, the party or attorney advising that conduct, or both to pay the movant's reasonable expenses incurred in making the motion, including attorney's fees. But the court must not order this payment if:

  (i) the movant filed the motion before attempting in good faith to obtain the disclosure or discovery without court action;

  (ii) the opposing party's nondisclosure, response, or objection was substantially justified; or

  (iii) other circumstances make an award of expenses unjust.

 (B) *If the Motion Is Denied.* If the motion is denied, the court may issue any protective order authorized under Rule 26(c) and must, after giving an opportunity to be heard, require the movant, the attorney filing the motion, or both to pay the party or deponent who opposed the motion its reasonable expenses incurred in opposing the motion, including attorney's fees. But the court must not order this payment if the motion was substantially justified or other circumstances make an award of expenses unjust.

 (C) *If the Motion Is Granted in Part and Denied in Part.* If the motion is granted in part and denied in part, the court may issue any protective order authorized under Rule 26(c) and may, after giving an opportunity to be heard, apportion the reasonable expenses for the motion.

(b) **Failure to Comply with a Court Order.**

(1) *Sanctions Sought in the District Where the Deposition Is Taken.* If the court where the discovery is taken orders a deponent to be sworn or to answer a question and the deponent fails to obey, the failure may be treated as contempt of court. If a

deposition-related motion is transferred to the court where the action is pending, and that court orders a deponent to be sworn or to answer a question and the deponent fails to obey, the failure may be treated as contempt of either the court where the discovery is taken or the court where the action is pending.

(2) *Sanctions Sought in the District Where the Action Is Pending.*

(A) *For Not Obeying a Discovery Order.* If a party or a party's officer, director, or managing agent—or a witness designated under Rule 30(b)(6) or 31(a)(4)—fails to obey an order to provide or permit discovery, including an order under Rule 26(f), 35, or 37(a), the court where the action is pending may issue further just orders. They may include the following:

(i) directing that the matters embraced in the order or other designated facts be taken as established for purposes of the action, as the prevailing party claims;

(ii) prohibiting the disobedient party from supporting or opposing designated claims or defenses, or from introducing designated matters in evidence;

(iii) striking pleadings in whole or in part;

(iv) staying further proceedings until the order is obeyed;

(v) dismissing the action or proceeding in whole or in part;

(vi) rendering a default judgment against the disobedient party; or

(vii) treating as contempt of court the failure to obey any order except an order to submit to a physical or mental examination.

(B) *For Not Producing a Person for Examination.* If a party fails to comply with an order under Rule 35(a) requiring it to produce another person for examination, the court may issue any of the orders listed in Rule 37(b)(2)(A)(i)-(vi), unless the disobedient party shows that it cannot produce the other person.

(C) *Payment of Expenses.* Instead of or in addition to the orders above, the court must order the disobedient party, the attorney advising that party, or both to pay the reasonable expenses, including attorney's fees, caused by the failure, unless the failure was substantially justified or other circumstances make an award of expenses unjust.

(c) Failure to Disclose, to Supplement an Earlier Response, or to Admit.

(1) *Failure to Disclose or Supplement.* If a party fails to provide information or identify a witness as required by Rule 26(a) or (e), the party is not allowed to use that information or witness to supply evidence on a motion, at a hearing, or at a trial, unless the failure was substantially justified or is harmless. In addition to or instead of this sanction, the court, on motion and after giving an opportunity to be heard:

(A) may order payment of the reasonable expenses, including attorney's fees, caused by the failure;

(B) may inform the jury of the party's failure; and

(C) may impose other appropriate sanctions, including any of the orders listed in Rule 37(b)(2)(A)(i)-(vi).

(2) *Failure to Admit.* If a party fails to admit what is requested under Rule 36 and if the requesting party later proves a document to be genuine or the matter true, the requesting party may move that the party who failed to admit pay the reasonable expenses, including attorney's fees, incurred in making that proof. The court must so order unless:

(A) the request was held objectionable under Rule 36(a);

(B) the admission sought was of no substantial importance;

(C) the party failing to admit had a reasonable ground to believe that it might prevail on the matter; or

(D) there was other good reason for the failure to admit.

(d) Party's Failure to Attend Its Own Deposition, Serve Answers to Interrogatories, or Respond to a Request for Inspection.

(1) *In General.*

(A) *Motion; Grounds for Sanctions.* The court where the action is pending may, on motion, order sanctions if:

(i) a party or a party's officer, director, or managing agent—or a person designated under Rule 30(b)(6) or 31(a)(4)—fails, after being served with proper notice, to appear for that person's deposition; or

(ii) a party, after being properly served with interrogatories under Rule 33 or a request for inspection under Rule 34, fails to serve its answers, objections, or written response.

(B) *Certification.* A motion for sanctions for failing to answer or respond must include a certification that the movant has in good faith conferred or attempted to confer with the party failing to act in an effort to obtain the answer or response without court action.

(2) *Unacceptable Excuse for Failing to Act.* A failure described in Rule 37(d)(1)(A) is not excused on the ground that the discovery sought was objectionable, unless the party failing to act has a pending motion for a protective order under Rule 26(c).

(3) *Types of Sanctions.* Sanctions may include any of the orders listed in Rule 37(b)(2)(A)(i)-(vi). Instead of or in addition to these sanctions, the court must require the party failing to act, the attorney advising that party, or both to pay the reasonable expenses, including attorney's fees, caused by the failure, unless the failure was substantially justified or other circumstances make an award of expenses unjust.

[Text of subdivision (e) effective until December 1, 2015, absent contrary Congressional action.]

(e) **Failure to Provide Electronically Stored Information.** Absent exceptional circumstances, a court may not impose sanctions under these rules on a party for failing to provide electronical-ly stored information lost as a result of the routine, good-faith operation of an electronic information system.

[Text of subdivision (e) effective December 1, 2015, absent contrary Congressional action.]

(e) **Failure to Preserve Electronically Stored Information.** If electronically stored information that should have been preserved in the anticipation or conduct of litigation is lost because a party failed to take reasonable steps to preserve it, and it cannot be restored or replaced through additional discovery, the court:

(1) upon finding prejudice to another party from loss of the information, may order measures no greater than necessary to cure the prejudice; or

(2) only upon finding that the party acted with the intent to deprive another party of the information's use in the litigation may:

(A) presume that the lost information was unfavorable to the party;

(B) instruct the jury that it may or must presume the information was unfavorable to the party; or

(C) dismiss the action or enter a default judgment.

(f) **Failure to Participate in Framing a Discovery Plan.** If a party or its attorney fails to participate in good faith in developing and submitting a proposed discovery plan as required by Rule 26(f), the court may, after giving an opportunity to be heard, require that party or attorney to pay to any other party the reasonable expenses, including attorney's fees, caused by the failure.

(Amended December 29, 1948, effective October 20, 1949; March 30, 1970, effective July 1, 1970; April 29, 1980, effective August 1, 1980; amended by Pub.L. 96–481, Title II, § 205(a), October 21, 1980, 94 Stat. 2330, effective October 1, 1981; amended March 2, 1987, effective August 1, 1987; April 22, 1993, effective December 1, 1993; April 17, 2000, effective December 1, 2000; April 12, 2006, effective December 1, 2006; April 30, 2007, effective December 1, 2007; April 16, 2013, effective December 1, 2013; April 29, 2015, effective December 1, 2015, absent contrary Congressional action.)

TITLE VII. JUDGMENT

RULE 55. DEFAULT; DEFAULT JUDGMENT

(a) **Entering a Default.** When a party against whom a judgment for affirmative relief is sought has failed to plead or otherwise defend, and that failure is shown by affidavit or otherwise, the clerk must enter the party's default.

(b) **Entering a Default Judgment.**

(1) *By the Clerk.* If the plaintiff's claim is for a sum certain or a sum that can be made certain by computation, the clerk—on the plaintiff's request, with an affidavit showing the amount due—must enter judgment for that amount and costs against a defendant who has been defaulted for not appearing and who is neither a minor nor an incompetent person.

(2) *By the Court.* In all other cases, the party must apply to the court for a default judgment. A default judgment may be entered against a minor or incompetent person only if represented by a general guardian, conservator, or other like fiduciary who has appeared. If the party against whom a default judgment is sought has appeared personally or by a representative, that party or its representative must be served with written notice of the application at least 7 days before the hearing. The court may conduct hearings or make referrals—preserving any federal statutory right to a jury trial—when, to enter or effectuate judgment, it needs to:

(A) conduct an accounting;

(B) determine the amount of damages;

(C) establish the truth of any allegation by evidence; or

(D) investigate any other matter.

[Text of subdivision (c) effective until December 1, 2015, absent contrary Congressional action.]

(c) **Setting Aside a Default or a Default Judgment.** The court may set aside an entry of default for good cause, and it may set aside a default judgment under Rule 60(b).

[Text of subdivision (c) effective December 1, 2015, absent contrary Congressional action.]

(c) **Setting Aside a Default or a Default Judgment.** The court may set aside an entry of default for good cause, and it may set aside a final default judgment under Rule 60(b).

(d) **Judgment Against the United States.** A default judgment may be entered against the United States, its officers, or its agencies only if the claimant establishes a claim or right to relief by evidence that satisfies the court.

(Amended March 2, 1987, effective August 1, 1987; April 30, 2007, effective December 1, 2007; March 26, 2009, effective December 1, 2009; April 29, 2015, effective December 1, 2015, absent contrary Congressional action.)

TITLE XI. GENERAL PROVISIONS

RULE 84. FORMS

[Text of Rule 84 effective until December 1, 2015, absent contrary Congressional action.]

The forms in the Appendix suffice under these rules and illustrate the simplicity and brevity that these rules contemplate.

[Text of Rule 84 effective December 1, 2015, absent contrary Congressional action.]

[Abrogated (Apr. ___, 2015, eff. Dec. 1, 2015).]

(Amended December 27, 1946, effective March 19, 1948; April 30, 2007, effective December 1, 2007; April 29, 2015, effective December 1, 2015, absent contrary Congressional action.)

APPENDIX OF FORMS

[Publisher's Note: Absent contrary Congressional action, the Appendix of Forms will be abrogated and the text of Forms 5 and 6 will be directly incorporated into Rule 4, effective December 1, 2015. For text of the current forms, effective until December 1, 2015, see main pamphlet.]

UNITED STATES DISTRICT COURT FOR THE NORTHERN DISTRICT OF ILLINOIS

Including Amendments Received Through
August 1, 2015

LOCAL GENERAL RULES

LR 16.1 STANDING ORDER ESTABLISHING PRETRIAL PROCEDURE

(Adopted Pursuant to General Order of 26 June 1985; Amended Pursuant to General Orders of 27 November 1991 and 9 March 1995)

1. Introduction. This pretrial procedure is intended to secure a just, speedy, and inexpensive determination of the issues. If the type of procedure described below does not appear calculated to achieve these ends in this case, counsel should seek an immediate conference with the judge and opposing counsel so that alternative possibilities may be discussed. Failure of either party to comply with the substance or the spirit of this *Standing Order* may result in dismissal of the action, default or other sanctions appropriate under Fed. R. Civ. P. 16 or 37, 28 U.S.C. § 1927 or any other applicable provisions.

Parties should also be aware that there may be variances in the forms and procedures used by each of the judges in implementing these procedures. Accordingly, parties should contact the minute clerk for the assigned judge for a copy of any standing order of that judge modifying these procedures.

2. Scheduling Conference. Within 60 days after the appearance of a defendant and within 90 days after the complaint has been served on a defendant in each civil case (other than categories of cases excepted by local Civil Rule 16.1), the court will usually set a scheduling conference (ordinarily in the form of a status hearing) as required by Fed.R.Civ.P. 16. At the conference, counsel should be *fully prepared* and have authority to discuss any questions regarding the case, including questions raised by the pleadings, jurisdiction, venue, pending motions, motions contemplated to be filed, the contemplated joinder of additional parties, the probable length of time needed for discovery and the possibility of settlement of the case. Counsel will have the opportunity to discuss any problems confronting them, including the need for time in which to prepare for trial.

3. Procedures for Complex or Protracted Discovery. If at any time during the scheduling conference or later status, hearings it appears that complex or protracted discovery will be sought, the court may

(a) determine that the *Manual on Complex Litigation 2d* be used as a guide for procedures to be followed in the case, or

(b) determine that discovery should proceed by phases, or

(c) require that the parties develop a joint written discovery plan under Fed. R.Civ.P. 26 (f).

If the court elects to proceed with phased discovery, the first phase will address information necessary to evaluate the case, lay the foundation for a motion to dismiss or transfer, and explore settlement. At the end of the first phase, the court may require the parties to develop a joint written discovery plan under Fed.R.Civ.P. 26 (f) and this *Standing Order*.

If the court requires parties to develop a discovery plan, such plan shall be as specific as possible concerning dates, time, and places discovery will be sought and as to the names of persons whose depositions will be taken. It shall also specify the parties' proposed discovery closing date. Once approved by the court, the plan may be amended only for good cause. Where the parties are unable to agree on a joint discovery plan, each shall submit a plan to the court. After reviewing the separate plans, the court may take such action as it deems appropriate to develop the plan.

Where appropriate, the court may also set deadlines for filing and a time framework for the disposition of motions.

4. Discovery Closing Date. In cases subject to this *Standing Order,* the court will, at an appropriate point, set a discovery closing date. Except to the extent specified by the court on motion of either party, discovery must be *completed* before the discovery closing date. Discovery requested before the discovery closing date, but not scheduled for completion before the discovery closing date, does not comply with this order.

5. Settlement. Counsel and the parties are directed to undertake a good faith effort to settle that includes a thorough exploration of the prospects of settlement before undertaking the extensive labor of preparing the Order provided for in the next paragraph. The court may require that representatives of the parties with authority to bind them in settlement discussions be present or available by telephone during any settlement conference.

If the parties wish the court to participate in a settlement conference, counsel should ask the court or the minute clerk to schedule such conference. In a case where the trial will be conducted without a jury, particularly as the case nears the date set for trial, the preferred method of having the court preside over settlement talks is for the assigned judge to arrange for another judge to preside or to refer the task to a magistrate judge. If the case has not been settled and is placed on the court's trial calendar, settlement possibilities should continue to be explored throughout the period before trial. If the case is settled, counsel shall notify the minute clerk promptly and notice up the case for final order.

6. Final Pretrial Order. The court will schedule dates for submission of a proposed final pretrial order (Order) and final pretrial conference (Conference) in accordance with Fed.R.Civ.P. 16. In the period between notice and the date for submission of the pretrial order:

(a) Counsel for all parties are directed to meet in order to (1) reach agreement on any possible stipulations narrowing the issues of law and fact, (2) deal with nonstipulated issues in the manner stated in this paragraph and (3) exchange copies of documents that will be offered in evidence at the trial. The court may direct that counsel meet in person (face-to-face). It shall be the duty of counsel for plaintiff to initiate that meeting and the duty of other counsel to respond to plaintiff's counsel and to offer their full cooperation and assistance to fulfill both the substance and spirit of this standing order. If, after reasonable effort, any party cannot obtain the cooperation of other counsel, it shall be his or her duty to advise the court of this fact by appropriate means.

(b) Counsel s meeting shall be held sufficiently in advance of the date of the scheduled Conference with the court so that counsel for each party can furnish all other counsel with a statement (Statement) of the issues the party will offer evidence to support. The Statement will (1) eliminate any issues that appear in the pleadings about which there is no controversy, and (2) include all issues of law as well as ultimate issues of fact from the standpoint of each party.

(c) It is the obligation of counsel for plaintiff to prepare from the Statement a draft Order for submission to opposing counsel. Included in plaintiff's obligation for preparation of the Order is submission of it to opposing counsel in ample time for revision and timely filing. Full cooperation and assistance of all other counsel are required for proper preparation of the Order to fulfill both the substance and spirit of this Standing Order. All counsel will jointly submit the original and one copy of the final draft of the Order to the judge's chambers (or in open court, if so directed) on the date fixed for submission.

(d) All instructions and footnotes contained within the Final Pretrial Order form promulgated with this *Standing Order* must be followed. They will be binding on the parties at trial in the same manner as though repeated in the Order. If any counsel believes that any of the instructions and/or footnotes allow for any part of the Order to be deferred until after the Order itself is filed, that counsel shall file a motion seeking leave of court for such deferral.

(e) Any pending motions requiring determination in advance of trial (including, without limitation, motions in limine, disputes over specific jury instructions or the admissibility of any evidence at trial upon which the parties desire to present authorities and argument to the court) shall be specifically called to the court's attention not later than the date of submission of the Order.

(f) Counsel must consider the following matters during their conference:

(1) Jurisdiction (if any question exists in this respect, it must be identified in the Order);

(2) Propriety of parties; correctness of identity of legal entities; necessity for appointment of guardian, administrator, executor or other fiduciary, and validity of appointment if already made; correctness of designation of party as partnership, corporation or individual d/b/a trade name; and

(3) Questions of misjoinder or nonjoinder of parties.

7. Final Pretrial Conference. At the Conference each party shall be represented by the attorneys who will try the case (unless before the conference the court grants permission for other counsel to attend in their place). All attending attorneys will familiarize themselves with the pretrial rules and will come to the Conference with full authority to accomplish the purposes of F.R.Civ.P. 16 (including simplifying the issues, expediting the trial and saving expense to litigants). Counsel shall be prepared to discuss settlement possibilities at the Conference without the necessity of obtaining confirmatory authorization from their clients. If a party represented by counsel desires to be present at the Conference, that party's counsel must notify the adverse parties at least one week in advance of the conference. If a party is not going to be present at the Conference, that party's counsel shall use their best efforts to provide that the client can be contacted if necessary. Where counsel represents a governmental body, the court may for good cause shown authorize that counsel to attend the Conference even if unable to enter into settlement without consultation with counsel s client.

8. Extensions of Time for Final Pretrial Order or Conference. It is essential that parties adhere to the scheduled dates for the Order and Conference, for the Conference date governs the case's priority for trial. Because of the scarcity of Conference dates, courtesy to counsel in other cases also mandates no late changes in scheduling. Accordingly, *no* extensions of

the Order and Conference dates will be granted without good cause, and no request for extension should be made less than 14 days before the scheduled Conference.

9. Action Following Final Pretrial Conference. At the conclusion of the Conference the court will enter an appropriate order reflecting the action taken, and the case will be added to the civil trial calendar. Although no further pretrial conference will ordinarily be held thereafter, a final conference may be requested by any of the parties or ordered by the court prior to trial. Any case ready for trial will be subject to trial as specified by the court.

10. Documents Promulgated with the *Standing Order.* Appended to this *Standing Order* are the following:

(a) a form of final pretrial order;

(b) a form for use as Schedule (c), the schedule of exhibits for the final pretrial order;

(c) a form of pretrial memorandum to be attached to the completed final pretrial order in personal injury cases;

(d) a form of pretrial memorandum to be attached to the completed final pretrial order in employment discrimination cases; and 9

(e) guidelines for preparing proposed findings of fact and conclusions of law.

Each of the forms is annotated to indicate the manner in which it is to be completed.

[Effective June 26, 1985. Amended effective November 27, 1991; March 9, 1995.]

LR 16.1.1 PRETRIAL PROCEDURES

(a) **Standing Order & Form.** Pursuant to Fed.R.Civ.P. 16, the Court has adopted a standing order on pretrial procedures together with model pretrial order forms. Copies of the standing order and forms shall be available from the clerk [see appendix]. The procedures set forth in the standing order, except for the need to prepare the pretrial order itself, shall apply to all civil cases except for those in categories enumerated in section (b) of this rule. As to all other cases, a pretrial order shall be prepared whenever the judge to whom a case is assigned so orders.

(b) Exempted Classes of Cases. The pretrial procedures adopted pursuant to section (a) of this rule shall not apply to the following classes of civil cases (The statistical nature of suit ("NS") codes are shown in parentheses following the class of cases.):

(1) Recovery of overpayments and student loan cases (NS: 150, 152, 153);

(2) Mortgage foreclosure cases (NS: 220);

(3) Prisoner petitions (NS: 510, 520, 530, 540, 550);

(4) U.S. forfeiture/penalty cases (NS: 610, 620, 630, 640, 650, 660, 690);

(5) Bankruptcy appeals and transfers (NS: 420, 421

(6) Deportation reviews (NS: 460);

(7) ERISA: Collections of Delinquent Contributions;

(8) Social Security reviews (NS: 861, 862, 863, 864, 865);

(9) Tax suits & IRS third party (NS: 870, 871);

(10) Customer challenges 12 U.S.C. § 3410 (NS: 875); or

(11) Cases brought under the Agricultural Acts, Economic Stabilization Act, Energy Allocation Act, Freedom of Information Act, Appeal of Fee Determination Under Equal Access to Justice Act, NARA Title II (NS: 891, 892, 894, 895, 900, 970)

Not withstanding the provisions of this rule, a pretrial order shall be prepared whenever the judge to whom a case is assigned so orders.

[Former Local Rule 16.1 adopted June 26, 1985 and amended effective November 27, 1991; March 9, 1995; and October 4, 2006. Renumbered and amended effective June 29, 2015.]

LR 48.1   CONTACT WITH JURORS

After the conclusion of a trial, no party, agent or attorney shall communicate or attempt to communicate with any members of the petit jury before which the case was tried without first receiving permission of the court.

[Effective April 27, 2015.]

LR 81.4   HABEAS CORPUS PROCEEDINGS IN DEPORTATION CASES

(a) Appeal From Immigration Judge. Where an appeal from an order of an Immigration Judge is permitted by law, the petition must show that the alien has taken such an appeal to the Board of Immigration Appeals and that the appeal has been denied.

(b) Petition. In complying with the requirements of 28 U.S.C. § 2242, the petitioner shall specify the acts which have deprived the petitioner of a fair hearing or other reasons entitling petitioner to the relief sought. To the extent practicable, the petition shall state the following:

(1) that the facts recited have been obtained from the records of the Department of Homeland Security; or

(2) that access to such records has been refused, in which event the petition shall state when and by whom application was made and refused; or

(3) that the interval between the notice of removal and the date of removal is too short to allow an examination of the records.

The petition shall further set forth the dates of the notice and the affirmance of the orders, the date set for departure, and the basis for inability to make the necessary examination.

(c) Service of Writ and Stay of Order. The writ shall be addressed to, and must be personally served upon, the officer who has actual physical custody of the alien. Service may not be made upon a master after a ship has cast off her moorings. Service may be not be made upon a captain of an aircraft after an alien has boarded the aircraft and the aircraft door is closed. Service of the writ does not stay the removal of an alien pending the court's decision on the writ, unless the court orders otherwise.

[Effective September 1, 1999. Amended effective January 31, 2000; May 27, 2015.]

LR 83.11   TRIAL BAR

(a) Definitions. The following definitions shall apply to this rule:

(1) The term "testimonial proceedings" refers to proceedings that meet all of the following criteria:

(A) they are evidentiary proceedings in which all testimony is given under oath and a record is made of the testimony;

(B) the witness or witnesses are subject to cross-examination;

(C) a presiding officer is present;

(D) the parties to such proceedings are generally represented by attorneys; and

(E) where a proceeding was held before an administrative agency, the findings and determinations of the agency are based upon the proceeding and are reviewable for sufficiency of evidence by a court of record.

Procedures limited to taking the deposition of a witness do not constitute testimonial proceedings for the purposes of this rule.

(2) The term "qualifying trial" refers to an evidentiary proceeding that meets the following criteria:

(A) it lasts at least one day;

(B) it must be a trial or hearing involving substantial testimonial proceedings going to the merits; and

(C) it must be held in open court before one of the following: a judge or magistrate judge of a United States district court; a judge of a United States bankruptcy court; a judge of the United States Tax Court; a judge of a trial court of record of a state, the District of Columbia, or a territory of the United States; or any administrative law judge.

(3) The term "participation units" shall mean a qualifying trial in which the petitioner participated as the lead counsel or the assistant to the lead counsel.

(4) The term "observation unit" shall mean a qualifying trial the petitioner observed while being supervised by a supervising attorney who consulted with the observer about the trial. At the time of the observation the supervising attorney must either have been a member of the trial bar of this Court or have had previous trial experience equivalent to at least 4 participation units.

(5) The term "simulation unit" shall mean a trial advocacy program in which the focus is experiential, as contrasted to lecture in which the petitioner satisfactorily participated either as a law school or a continuing legal education course.

(6) The term "training unit of the District Court" shall mean participation in a training seminar officially sanctioned by the Court.

(7) The term "qualifying unit of trial experience" shall include any of the following: participation units, observation units, simulation units, and training units. A petitioner shall be credited the following qualifying units of trial experience for the experience indicated:

(A) for each participation unit, 2 units where the trial lasted 9 days or less, 3 units where the trial lasted from 10 to 12 full days, and 4 units where the trial lasted 13 or more full days;

(B) for each observation unit, 1 unit;

(C) for each simulation unit, 2 units; and

(D) for each training unit of the District Court, 1 unit.

(8) The term "required trial experience" shall mean not less than 4 qualifying units of trial experience.

(9) The term "pro bono panel" shall refer to a panel of members of the trial bar selected pursuant to LR83.35(b) for the purpose of representing or assisting in the representation of parties unable to afford to hire a member of the trial bar.

(NOTE: See Regulations Pertaining to Trial Bar Admissions for additional material relating to admissions. The Regulations are located in the Appendix to the local Rules.)

(b) Qualifications. An applicant for admission to the trial bar of this Court must be a member in good standing of the general bar of this Court and provide evidence of having the required trial experience. Anyone wishing to apply for admission to the trial bar who is not a member of the bar of this Court may apply for admission to both bars simultaneously.

(c) Petition Form. The Executive Committee will approve a form of petition to be used by anyone applying for admission to the trial bar. Copies of the approved form will be provided on request by the clerk.

(d) Screening the Petition. The clerk, under the supervision of the Executive Committee, will screen each petition to assure that it is filed on the correct form, has been completed, and contains sufficient information to establish that the petitioner meets the qualifications required for the trial bar. Where these requirements are met, an indication to that effect will be placed on the petition and the petitioner will be notified that the petition is approved. Where the requirements are not met, the petition will be returned to the applicant with appropriate instructions.

(e) Admission Fee. Each petitioner shall pay an admission fee upon the filing of the petition, provided that in the event the petitioner is not admitted, the petitioner may request that the fee be refunded. The amount of the fee shall be established by the court.

The clerk shall deposit the fee in the District Court Fund.

(f) Duty to Supervise. Every member of the trial bar shall be available to be assigned by the court to supervise attorneys who are in the process of obtaining observation units needed to qualify for membership in the trial bar. Such assignments shall be made in a manner so as to allocate the responsibility imposed by this rule equally among all members of the trial bar.

(g) Duty to Accept Assignments. Each member of the trial bar shall be available for assignment by the court to represent or assist in the representation of those who cannot afford to hire a member of the trial bar. Assignments under this rule shall be made in a manner such that no member of the trial bar shall be required to accept more than one assignment during any 12 month period.

(h) Withdrawal from Trial Bar. A member of the trial bar may, on motion for good cause shown, voluntarily withdraw from said bar. Such motion shall be filed with the clerk for presentation to the Executive Committee. Where the motion to withdraw is made by a member of the current pro bono panel the name of the attorney will be removed from the pro bono panel if the motion is granted.

(i) Reinstatement. Any attorney permitted to withdraw as a member of the trial bar pursuant to section (h) who wishes to be reinstated must file a petition for reinstatement with the clerk for presentation to the Executive Committee. Where the attorney was a member of a pro bono panel at the time the petition to withdraw was filed, the petition for reinstatement shall include a statement indicating the attorney's present willingness and ability to accept an assignment under LR83.35 through LR83.41. If the committee grants the motion in such an instance, it shall direct that the attorney be included in the pro bono panel and remain there for one year or until the attorney is assigned, whichever comes first.

[Effective September 1, 1999. Amended effective June 24, 2009; November 2, 2010; May 24, 2013; May 27, 2015; June 29, 2015.]

LR 83.40 EXPENSES

The party shall bear the cost of any expenses of the litigation or appeal to the extent reasonably feasible in light of the party's financial condition. Such expenses shall include, but not be limited to discovery expenses, subpoena and witness fees, and transcript expenses. It shall be permissible for assigned counsel or the firm with which counsel is affiliated to advance part or all of the payment of any such expenses without requiring that the party remain ultimately liable for such expenses, except out of the proceeds of any recovery. However, the attorney or firm shall not be required to advance the payment of such expenses.

Expenses incurred by counsel assigned pursuant to LR83.36 or the firm with which counsel is affiliated may be reimbursed from the District Court Fund in accordance with the provisions of the *Regulations Governing the Reimbursement of Expenses in Pro Bono Cases*. The clerk will provide copies of the *Regulations* and the *Plan for the Administration of the District Court Fund* on request.

[Effective September 1, 1999. Amended effective June 30, 2015.]

LR 83.41 ATTORNEY'S FEES

(a) Party's Ability to Pay. Where as part of the process of assigning counsel the judge finds that the party is able to pay for legal services in whole or in part but that assignment is justified, the judge shall include in the order of assignment provisions for any fee arrangement between the party and the assigned counsel.

If assigned counsel discovers after assignment that the party is able to pay for legal services in whole or in part, counsel shall bring that information to the attention of the judge. Thereupon the judge may either (1) authorize the party and counsel to enter into a fee agreement subject to the judge's approval, or (2) relieve counsel from the responsibilities of the order of assignment and either permit the party to retain an attorney or to proceed pro se.

(b) Fee Agreements. If assigned counsel wishes to negotiate a fee arrangement with the client, counsel must do so at the outset of the representation. Any such fee arrangement is subject to all applicable rules and canons of professional conduct. Any fee agreement that assigned counsel and the client may reach must be submitted to the court for review and approval before the agreement becomes effective, and is subject to revision by the court.

(c) Allowance of Fees. Upon appropriate application by assigned counsel, the judge may award attorney's fees to assigned counsel for services rendered in the action as authorized by applicable statute, regulation, rule, or other provision of law, including case law.

[Effective September 1, 1999. Amended effective January 31, 2012; June 29, 2015.]

LOCAL CRIMINAL RULES

LCrR 41. SEARCH WARRANTS

(a) Submission of Warrant Applications. Except for matters that are reserved for the Chief Judge (for example, in LCr 50.2 (2) and LCr 6.1) and as provided in (b), applications for search warrants or seizure warrants must be submitted to the duty magistrate judge.

(b) A district judge may issue a standing order that search warrants or seizure warrants related to a case assigned to that judge must be brought to that judge.

(c) Assignment of ease numbers. When an application for a search warrant or seizure warrant is approved and the warrant is signed by the duty magistrate judge, the application and warrant will be given a Miscellaneous (M) case number and be assigned to the magistrate judge who signed the, warrant. When a search warrant or seizure warrant is signed by a district judge as provided in (b), the application and warrant will be given the CR number of the case before the district judge and docketed in that case.

(d) Motions to Seal. This rule, rather than LR 26.2, governs a motion to seal a search warrant or seizure warrant. A motion to seal a warrant must be brought to the district judge or magistrate judge who signed the warrant, and must specify a date no more than 90 days later when the sealing order will expire absent a further court order. Any application for delayed notice of a search must comply with 18 U.S.C. § 3103. All filings will be unsealed upon the expiration of the sealing order.

(e) A Motion to Extend a Sealing Order.

(1) Any motion to extend an order sealing a warrant or to extend delayed notice must be brought to the district judge or magistrate judge who signed the warrant. If a motion is brought at a time when that judge is unavailable, the motion shall be heard by the duty magistrate judge.

(2) The motion must be filed no later than three days prior to the expiration of the seal or delayed notice to allow adequate time for the review of the motion. The motion shall be filed electronically and a draft order must be submitted to the assigned judge's proposed order email box.

(f) Search Warrant Returns. The return of the search warrant must be made in accordance with the Federal Rules of Criminal Procedure. In addition to that requirement, the United States Attorney's Office must also electronically tile a copy of the return including the inventory of property seized into the court's Electronic Case Filing System. If the application and warrant are sealed at the time of the return of the search warrant, the return of the search warrant will also be filed under seal.

[Effective April 27, 2015.]

APPENDICES

APPENDIX A.　STANDING PRETRIAL PROCEDURE ORDER AND FORMS

FORM LR 16.1.4　FINAL PRETRIAL ORDER FORM

IN THE UNITED STATES DISTRICT COURT
FOR THE NORTHERN DISTRICT OF ILLINOIS
[*indicate Eastern or Western*] DIVISION

Plaintiff,[1]	)	
	)	
	)	
v.	)	Civil Action No.
	)	
	)	
Defendant.	)	Judge [*Insert name of*
	)	assigned judge*]*

FINAL PRETRIAL ORDER

This matter having come before the court at a pretrial conference held pursuant to Fed. R. Civ. P. ("Rule") 16, and [*insert name, address and telephone number*] having appeared as counsel for plaintiff(s) and [*insert name, address and telephone number*] having appeared as counsel for defendant(s), the following actions were taken:

(1) This is an action for [*insert nature of action, e.g., breach of contract, personal injury*] and the jurisdiction of the court is invoked under [*insert citation of statute on which jurisdiction based*].　Jurisdiction is (not) disputed.[2]

(2) The following stipulations and statements were submitted and are attached to and made a part of this Order:[3]

(a) a comprehensive stipulation or statement of all uncontested facts, which will become a part of the evidentiary record in the case (and which, in jury trials, may be read to the jury by the court or any party);[4]

(b) for jury trials a short agreed description of the case to be read to prospective jurors.

(c) except for rebuttal exhibits, schedules in the form set out in the attached Schedule (c) of—

　(1) all exhibits (all exhibits shall be marked for identification before trial), including documents, summaries, charts and other items expected to be offered in evidence and

　(2) any demonstrative evidence and experiments to be offered during trial;[5]

(d) a list or lists of names and addresses of the potential witnesses to be called by each party, with a statement of any objections to calling, or to the qualifications of, any witness identified on the list;[6]

(e) stipulations or statements setting forth the qualifications of each F.R. Evid. 702 witness in such form that the statement can be read to the jury at the time the F.R. Evid. 702 witness takes the stand;[7]

(f) a list of all depositions, and designated page and line numbers, to be read into evidence and statements of any objections thereto;[8]

(g) an itemized statement of damages;

(h)* for a jury trial, each party shall provide the following:

　(i) trial briefs except as otherwise ordered by the court;[9]

(ii) one set of marked proposed jury instructions, verdict forms and special interrogatories, if any;[10] and

(iii) a list of the questions the party requests the court to ask prospective jurors in accordance with Fed.R.Civ.P. 47(a);

(i) a statement that each party has completed discovery, including the depositions of F.R. Evid. 702 witnesses (unless the court has previously ordered otherwise). Absent good cause shown, no further discovery shall be permitted;[11] and

(j) subject to full compliance with all the procedural requirements of Rule 37(a)(1), a brief summary of intended motions in limine. Any briefs in support of and responses to such motions shall be filed as directed by the Court.

(2.1) The following *optional* stipulations and statements were submitted and are attached to and made a part of this Order:

(k)* an agreed statement or statements by each party of the contested issues of fact and law and a statement or statements of contested issues of fact or law not agreed to;

(*l*)* waivers of any claims or defenses that have been abandoned by any party;

(m)* for a non-jury trial, each party shall provide proposed *Findings of Fact and Conclusions of Law* in duplicate (see guidelines available from the court's minute clerk or secretary);[12]

(3) Trial of this case is expected to take [*insert the number of days trial expected to take*] days. It will be listed on the trial calendar, to be tried when reached.

(4) [*Indicate the type of trial by placing an X in the appropriate box*]

     Jury ☐   Non-jury ☐

(5) The parties recommend that [*indicate the number of jurors recommended*][13] jurors be selected at the commencement of the trial.

(6) The parties [*insert "agree" or "do not agree" as appropriate*] that the issues of liability and damages [*insert "should" or "should not" as appropriate*] be bifurcated for trial. On motion of any party or on motion of the court, bifurcation may be ordered in either a jury or a non-jury trial.

(7) [*Pursuant to 28 U.S.C. § 636(c), parties may consent to the reassignment of this case to a magistrate judge who may conduct any or all proceedings in a jury or nonjury civil matter and order the entry of judgment in the case. Indicate below if the parties consent to such a reassignment.*]

     ☐ The parties consent to this case being reassigned to a magistrate judge for trial.

(8) This Order will control the course of the trial and may not be amended except by consent of the parties and the court, or by order of the court to prevent manifest injustice.

(9) Possibility of settlement of this case was considered by the parties.

                              _____
                                 United States District Judge[14]

Date: _____

[*Attorneys are to sign the form before presenting it to the court.*]

_____   _____
Attorney for Plaintiff   Attorney for Defendant

Schedule (c)

Exhibits[15]

1. The following exhibits were offered by plaintiff, received in evidence and marked as indicated:

[State identification number and brief description of each exhibit.]

2. The following exhibits were offered by plaintiff and marked for identification. Defendant(s) objected to their receipt in evidence on the grounds stated:[16]

[State identification number and brief description of each exhibit. Also state briefly the ground of objection, such as competency, relevancy or materiality, and the provision of Fed.R.Evid. relied upon. Also state briefly plaintiff's response to the objection, with appropriate reference to Fed.R.Evid.]

3. The following exhibits were offered by defendant, received in evidence and marked as indicated:

[State identification number and brief description of each exhibit.]

4. The following exhibits were offered by defendant and marked for identification. Plaintiff objected to their receipt in evidence on the grounds stated:[17]

[State identification number and brief description of each exhibit. Also state briefly the ground of objection, such as competency, relevancy or materiality, and the provision of Fed.R.Evid. relied upon. Also state briefly defendant's response to the objection, with appropriate reference to Fed.R.Evid.]

5. Non-objected-to exhibits are received in evidence by operation of this Order. However, in jury trials, exhibits that have not been explicitly referred to in testimony or otherwise published to the jury prior to the close of all evidence or in argument are not in evidence.

[1] Singular forms are used throughout this document. Plural forms should be used as appropriate. Where a third-party defendant is joined pursuant to Rule 14(a), the Order may be suitably modified. In such cases, the caption and the statement of parties and counsel shall be modified to reflect the joiner.

[2] In diversity cases or other cases requiring a jurisdictional amount in controversy, the Order shall contain either a stipulation that the required jurisdictional amount is involved or a brief written statement citing evidence supporting the claim that such sum could reasonably be awarded.

[3] The asterisked (*) options shall not be required unless the court explicitly orders inclusion of one or more of them. On motion of any party or on the court's own motion, any other requirement of the Order may be waived.

[4] Counsel for plaintiff has the responsibility to prepare the initial draft of a proposed stipulation dealing with allegations in the complaint. Counsel for any counter-, cross- or third-party complainant has the same responsibility to prepare a stipulation dealing with allegations in that party's complaints. If the admissibility of any uncontested fact is challenged, the party objecting and the grounds for objection must be stated.

[5] Items not listed will not be admitted unless good cause is shown. Cumulative documents, particularly x-rays and photos, shall be omitted. Duplicate exhibits shall not be scheduled by different parties, but may be offered as joint exhibits. All parties shall stipulate to the authenticity of exhibits whenever possible, and this Order shall identify any exhibits whose authenticity has not been stipulated to and specific reasons for the party's failure so to stipulate. As the attached Schedule (c) form indicates, non-objected-to exhibits which have been explicitly referred to in testimony or stipulation or published to the jury are received in evidence by operation of this Order, without any need for further foundation testimony. Copies of exhibits shall be made available to opposing counsel and a bench book of exhibits shall be prepared and delivered to the court at the start of the trial unless excused by the court. If the trial is a jury trial and counsel desires to display exhibits to the members of the jury, sufficient copies of such exhibits must be made available so as to provide each juror with a copy, or alternatively, enlarged photographic copies or projected copies should be used.

[6] Each party shall indicate which witnesses *will* be called in the absence of reasonable notice to opposing counsel to the contrary, and which *may* be called as a possibility only. Any witness not

listed will be precluded from testifying absent good cause shown, except that each party reserves the right to call such rebuttal witnesses (who are not presently identifiable) as may be necessary, without prior notice to the opposing party.

[7] Only one F.R. Evid. 702 witness on each subject for each party will be permitted to testify absent good cause shown. If more than one F.R. Evid. 702 witness is listed, the subject matter of each expert's testimony shall be specified.

[8] If any party objects to the admissibility of any portion, both the name of the party objecting and the grounds shall be stated. Additionally, the parties shall be prepared to present to the court, at such time as directed to do so, a copy of all relevant portions of the deposition transcript to assist the court in ruling *in limine* on the objection. All irrelevant and redundant material including all colloquy between counsel shall be eliminated when the deposition is read at trial. If a video deposition is proposed to be used, opposing counsel must be so advised sufficiently before trial to permit any objections to be made and ruled on by the court, to allow objectionable material to be edited out of the film before trial.

[9] (*Note: The use of the asterisk (*) is explained in Footnote 3.*) No party's trial brief shall exceed 15 pages without prior approval of the court. Trial briefs are intended to provide full and complete disclosure of the parties' respective theories of the case. Accordingly, each trial brief shall include statements of—

(a) the nature of the case,

(b) the contested facts the party expects the evidence will establish,

(c) the party's theory of liability or defense based on those facts and the uncontested facts,

(d) the party's theory of damages or other relief in the event liability is established, and

(e) the party's theory of any anticipated motion for directed verdict.

The brief shall also include citations of authorities in support of each theory stated in the brief. Any theory of liability or defense that is not expressed in a party's trial brief will be deemed waived.

[10] *Agreed* instructions shall be presented by the parties whenever possible. Whether agreed or unagreed, each marked copy of an instruction shall indicate the proponent and supporting authority and shall be numbered. All objections to tendered instructions shall be in writing and include citations of authorities. Failure to object may constitute a waiver of any objection.

In diversity and other cases where Illinois law provides the rules of decision, use of Illinois Pattern Instructions ("IPI") as to all issues of substantive law is required. As to all other issues, and as to all issues of substantive law where Illinois law does not control, the following pattern jury instructions shall be used in the order listed, e.g., an instruction from (b) shall be used only if no such instruction exists in (a):

(a) the Seventh Circuit pattern jury instructions; or,

(b) any pattern jury instructions published by a federal court. (Care should be taken to make certain substantive instructions on federal questions conform to Seventh Circuit case law.)

At the time of trial, an unmarked original set of instructions and any special interrogatories (on 8½″ × 11″ sheets) shall be submitted to the court; to be sent to the jury room after being read to the jury. Supplemental requests for instructions during the course of the trial or at the conclusion of the evidence will be granted solely as to those matters that cannot be reasonably anticipated at the time of presentation of the initial set of instructions.

[11] If this is a case in which (contrary to the normal requirements) discovery has not been completed, this Order shall state what discovery remains to be completed by each party.

[12] These shall be separately stated in separately numbered paragraphs. Findings of Fact should contain a detailed listing of the relevant material facts the party intends to prove. They should not be in formal language, but should be in simple narrative form. Conclusions of Law should contain concise statements of the meaning or intent of the legal theories set forth by counsel.

[13] Rule 48 specifies that a civil jury shall consist of not fewer than six nor more than twelve jurors.

[14] Where the case has been reassigned on consent of parties to a magistrate judge for all purposes, the magistrate judge will, of course, sign the final pretrial order.

[15] As in the Final Pretrial Order form, references to "plaintiff" and "defendant" are intended to cover those instances where there are more than one of either.

[16] Copies of objected-to exhibits should be delivered to the court with this Order, to permit rulings *in limine* where possible.

[17] *See* footnote 17. [**Publisher's Note:** So in original. Probably should be "16".]

[Former Form LR16.1.1, effective September 1, 1999. Amended effective July 1, 2008. Renumbered effective July 24, 2015.]

Committee Comment

The amendment to the Final Pretrial Order Form will improve efficiency in litigation.

UNITED STATES DISTRICT COURT FOR THE CENTRAL DISTRICT OF ILLINOIS

Including Amendments Received Through
August 1, 2015

GENERAL AND CIVIL RULES

RULE 5.7 ELECTRONIC FILING PROCEDURES

(A) Pleadings and Documents Other Than Case Initiating Documents. All motions, pleadings, applications, briefs, memoranda of law, exhibits, or other documents in a civil case (except for complaints) must be electronically filed on the System except as otherwise provided by these Rules.

(1) A document submitted electronically will not be considered filed for purposes of the Federal Rules of Civil Procedure until the System-generated Notice of Electronic Filing has been sent electronically to the filing party.

(2) E–mailing a document to the Clerk's Office or to the assigned judge does not constitute "filing" of the document.

(3) A document filed electronically by 11:59 p.m. central standard time will be deemed filed on that date.

(B) Case Initiating Documents.

(1) The Clerk's Office will accept case initiating documents (i.e. complaints with civil cover sheets and summons, and notices of removal) sent by e-mail or directly into the CM/ECF system.

(a) A party submitting a case initiating document by e-mail for electronic filing must submit those documents in .pdf format to the proper divisional mailbox, as follows:

newcases.peoria@ilcd.uscourts.gov
newcases.urbana@ilcd.uscourts.gov
newcases.springfield@ilcd.uscourts.gov
newcases.rockisland@ilcd.uscourts.gov

(b) Payment of the filing fee must be made by cash, cashier's check, law firm check, money order or credit card. Credit card payments may be made using pay.gov or by giving a credit card number, by phone, to the appropriate clerk's office.

(c) Case initiating documents submitted by e-mail will be deemed filed on the date that the complaint is received by e-mail or the date that the filing fee is paid, whichever is later.

(d) Case initiating documents filed by pro se plaintiffs will be deemed filed on the date received by the Clerk's Office. Legal issues regarding filing date or receipt of fees will be resolved by the Court.

(2) The Clerk's Office also will accept for filing case initiating documents sent by United States mail or delivered in person to the Clerk's Office when accompanied by the filing fee or a Petition to Proceed in forma pauperis. A case initiating document received in paper form will be scanned and uploaded by the Clerk's Office. Unless otherwise provided in these procedures, the paper documents will then be discarded.

(3) Only case initiating documents may be sent to the e-mail addresses listed above. If any other documents are sent to those e-mail addresses, the Clerk's Office will reply to the e-mail, notifying the party that the pleading has not been filed.

(4) A party may not electronically serve a case initiating document, but instead must effect service according to Fed. R. Civ. P. 4. Electronic service of a Notice of Filing does not constitute service of process where service of process is required by Fed. R. Civ. P. 4.

(C) Titling Docket Entries. The party electronically filing a pleading or other document is responsible for designating a docket entry title for the document by using one of the docket event categories prescribed by the court.

(D) Filing Problems.

(1) *Corrections.* Once a document is submitted and becomes part of the case docket, corrections to the docket are made only by the Clerk's Office. The System will not permit the filing party to make changes to the document or docket entry filed in error once the transaction has been accepted. The filing party should not attempt to refile a document. As soon as possible after an error is discovered, the filing party should contact the Clerk's Office with the case number and document number for which the correction is being requested. If appropriate, the Court will make an entry indicating that the document was filed in error. The filing party will be advised *if* the document needs to be refiled.

(2) *Technical Problems.*

(a) Technical Failures. The Clerk's Office will deem the Central District of Illinois CM/ECF site to be subject to a technical failure on a given day if the site is unable to accept filings continuously or intermittently over the course of any period of time greater than one hour after 10:00 a.m. that day. In the event a technical failure occurs, and despite the best efforts of the filing party a document cannot be filed electronically, the party should print (if possible) a copy of the error message received. As soon as possible, the party should file this message with a Declaration That Party Was Unable to File in a Timely Manner Due to Technical Difficulties.

(b) Filer's Problems. Problems on the filer's end, such as phone line problems, problems with the filer's Internet Service Provider (ISP) or hardware or software problems will neither constitute a technical failure nor excuse an untimely filing. If a party misses a filing deadline due to such problems, the document may be conventionally submitted, accompanied by a Declaration stating the reason for missing the deadline and a motion for leave to file instanter. The motion, document and declaration must be filed no later than 12:00 noon of the first day on which the Court is open for business following the original filing deadline. The Court will consider the matters stated in the declaration and order appropriate relief.

[Effective January 20, 2010. Amended effective June 1, 2015.]

RULE 7.1 MOTIONS

(A) Disposition of Motions: Oral Argument: Extension of Time.

(1) Any motion (other than summary judgment motions, which are governed by subparagraph (D) of this Rule) may, in the court's discretion, be:

(a) scheduled for oral argument, either at a specified time or on a Motion Day as suggested in Fed. R. Civ. P. 78;

(b) scheduled for determination by telephone conference call;

(c) referred to a United States magistrate judge for determination or recommendation; or

(d) determined upon the pleadings and the motion papers without benefit of oral argument.

(2) A party desiring oral argument on a motion filed under subparagraph (B) of this Rule must so specify in the motion or opposition thereto and must state the reason why oral argument is desired.

(3) Motions for extensions of time must be filed within the original time allowed.

(B) Memorandum of Law: Response; Reply; Length.

(1) Every motion raising a question of law (except summary judgment motions, which are governed by Subparagraph (D) of this Rule) must include a memorandum of law including a brief statement of the specific points or propositions of law and supporting authorities upon which the moving party relies, and identifying the Rule under which the motion is filed.

(2) Any party opposing a motion filed pursuant to (B)(1) must file a response to the motion, including a brief statement of the specific points or propositions of law and supporting authorities upon which the responding party relies. The response must be filed within 14 days after service of the motion and memorandum. If no response is timely filed, the presiding judge will presume there is no opposition to the motion and may rule without further notice to the parties.

(3) No reply to the response is permitted.

(4)(a) A memorandum in support of and in response to a motion must be double-spaced and must not exceed 15 pages in length, unless it complies with the following type volume limitation.

(b) A memorandum that exceeds 15 pages in length will comply with the type volume limitation if

(1) it does not contain more than 7000 words or 45,000 characters, or

(2) it uses monospaced type and does not contain more than 650 lines of text.

(c) A memorandum submitted under the type volume limitation must include a certificate by counsel, or by an unrepresented party, that the memorandum complies with the type volume limitation. The certificate of compliance must state the number of words, characters or lines of type in the memorandum. The person who prepares the certificate of compliance may rely on the word or character count of the word processing system used to prepare the document.

(d) All headings, footnotes, and quotations count toward the page, word, character, and line limitations.

(C) Supporting Documents. If documentary evidence is to be offered in support of or in opposition to a motion, and if that evidence is conveniently susceptible of copying, copies thereof will be served and filed by the moving party with the motion and by the opposing party with the response thereto. If the evidence is not susceptible of convenient copying, the offering party instead will furnish to the court and to the adverse party, a concise summary of the contents and will immediately make the original available to the adverse party for examination.

(D) Summary Judgment. All motions for summary judgment and responses and replies thereto must comply with the requirements of this rule. Any filings not in compliance may be stricken by the court. The consequences for failing to comply are discussed thoroughly in *Waldridge v. American Hoechst Corp.*, 24 F.3d 918 (7th Cir. 1994). Motions for extension of time to file a motion for summary judgment or a response to a reply thereto will not be looked upon with favor; such motions may be summarily denied unless they are filed within the original time as allowed by this rule or by the scheduling order.

(1) *Motion for Summary Judgment.* Any party filing a motion for summary judgment pursuant to Fed. R. Civ. P. 56 and the scheduling order entered in the case, must include in that motion the following sections with appropriate headings:

(a) Introduction. Without citations, briefly summarize the legal and factual basis for the motion and the exact relief sought.

(b) Undisputed Material Facts. List and number each undisputed material fact which is the basis for the motion for summary judgment. Include as exhibits to the motion all relevant documentary evidence. For each fact asserted, provide citations to the documentary evidence that supports it, appropriately referencing the exhibit and page.

A WORD OF CAUTION: Material facts are only those facts which bear directly on the legal issue raised by the motion.

(c) Argument. Under an appropriate subheading for each separate point of law, explain the legal point, with citations to authorities, and why or how the application of that point to the undisputed material facts entitles movant to the relief sought.

(2) *Response to Motion for Summary Judgment.* Within 21 days after service of a motion for summary judgment, any party opposing the motion must file a response. A failure to respond will be deemed an admission of the motion. The response must include the following sections with appropriate headings:

(a) Introduction. Without citations, briefly summarize the legal and factual basis for opposition to the motion and the exact relief sought.

(b) Response to Undisputed Material Facts. In separate subsections state the following:

(1) Undisputed material facts. List by number each fact from Section B of the motion for summary judgment which is conceded to be undisputed and material.

(2) Disputed Material Facts. List by number each fact from Section B of the motion for summary judgment which is conceded to be material but is claimed to be disputed. Each claim of disputed fact must be supported by evidentiary documentation referenced by specific page. Include as exhibits

all cited documentary evidence not already submitted by the movant.

(3) Disputed Immaterial Facts. List by number each fact from Section B of the motion for summary judgment which is claimed to be both immaterial and disputed. State the reason the fact is immaterial. Support the claim that the fact is disputed with evidentiary documentation referenced by specific page. Include as exhibits all cited documentary evidence not already submitted by the movant.

(4) Undisputed Immaterial Facts. List by number each fact from Section B of the motion for summary judgment which is undisputed but is claimed to be immaterial. State the reason the fact is immaterial.

(5) Additional Material Facts. List and number each additional material fact raised in opposition to the motion for summary judgment. Each additional fact must be supported by evidentiary documentation referenced by specific page. Include as exhibits all relevant documentary evidence not already submitted by the movant.

(6) A failure to respond to any numbered fact will be deemed an admission of the fact.

(c) Argument. With or without additional citations to authorities, respond directly to the argument in the motion for summary judgment, for example, by explaining any disagreement with the movant's explanation of each point of law, why a point of law does not apply to the undisputed material facts, why its application does not entitle movant to relief or why, for other reasons, summary judgment should not be granted.

(3) *Movant's Reply.* Within 14 days after service of response, the movant may file a reply. The reply must include the following subsections, appropriately titled:

(a) Reply to Additional Material Facts. List by number the additional facts asserted in Section (b)(5) of the response. For each fact, state succinctly whether:

(1) it is conceded to be material and undisputed,

(2) it is conceded to be material but is disputed, in which case provide support the claim that the fact is disputed

by providing citations to specific pages of evidentiary documentation. Include as exhibits all cited documentary evidence not already submitted,

(3) it is immaterial but disputed, in which case state the reason the the fact is immaterial and support the claim that the fact is disputed by providing citations to evidentiary documentation, attached as exhibits and referenced by specific page,

(4) it is immaterial and undisputed, in which case explain the reason it is immaterial,

(5) A failure to respond to any numbered fact will be deemed an admission of that fact.

(b) Argument. Succinctly and directly address any matters raised in the response with which the movant disagrees. THE REPLY WILL BE LIMITED TO NEW MATTERS RAISED IN THE RESPONSE AND MUST NOT RESTATE ARGUMENTS ALREADY RAISED IN THE MOTION.

(4) *Oral Arguments.* The Court may take the motion for summary judgment under advisement without oral argument or may schedule argument with appropriate notice to the parties. A party may file a request for oral argument and hearing at the time of filing either a motion or response pursuant to this Rule.

(5) *Page and Type Limitations.* Page and type volume limitations, as set forth in Rule 7.1(B)(4), apply to Section (1)(c) of the motion for summary judgment and to Section (2)(c) of the response to the motion. The argument section of a reply must not exceed five double-spaced pages in length.

(6) *Exceptions.* Local Rule 7.1(D) does not apply to social security appeals or any other case upon the showing of good cause.

(E) Amended Pleadings. Whenever an amended pleading is filed, any motion attacking the original pleading will be deemed moot unless specifically revived by the moving party within 14 days after the amended pleading is served.

[Effective January 20, 2010. Amended effective March 15, 2010; June 1, 2015.]

RULE 8.1   SOCIAL SECURITY CASES: REVIEW UNDER 42 U.S.C. § 405(g)

(A) Complaints: Contents. Any person seeking judicial review of a decision of the Commissioner of Social Security under Section 205(g) of the Social Security Act (42 U.S.C. § 405(g)) must provide, on a separate paper attached to the complaint served on the Commissioner of Social Security, the social security number of the worker on whose wage record the application for benefits was filed. The person must also state, in the complaint, that the social security number has been attached to the copy of the complaint served on the Commissioner of Social Security. Failure to provide a social security number to the Commissioner of Social Security will not be grounds for dismissal of the complaint.

(B) Complaints: Form of Allegation. In keeping with Fed. R. Civ. P. 84 and the Appendix of Forms to the Federal Rules of Civil Procedure, the following form of allegations in a complaint is considered sufficient for § 405(g) review cases in this court:

(1) The plaintiff is a _____ resident of

                (City and State)

(2) The plaintiff complains of a decision which adversely affects (him) (her). The decision has become the final decision of the Commissioner for purposes of judicial review and bears the following caption:

In the case of   Claim for

_____   _____

Claimant

_____

Wage Earner

(3) The plaintiff has exhausted administrative remedies in this matter and this court has jurisdiction for judicial review pursuant to 42 U.S.C. § 405(g).

WHEREFORE, plaintiff seeks judicial review by this court and the entry of judgment for such relief as may be proper, including costs.

(C) Service.

(1) Where a complaint for administrative review is filed pursuant to 42 U.S.C. Section 405(g) and plaintiff in that complaint is allowed to proceed in forma pauperis, then the United States Attorney and Social Security Administration agree that service of initial process (i.e. summons and complaint) upon the United States Attorney and Social Security Administration under Fed. R. Civ. P. 4(i)(1)(A and C) may be accomplished by electronic delivery of the summons and complaint through the court's Case Management and Electronic Filing System (CM/ECF) to e-mail addresses provided to the Clerk's Office by the United States Attorney. The United States Attorney and Social Security Administration will treat this electronic delivery of the summons and complaint as service under Fed. R.Civ.P. 4(i)(1)(A and C). Service on the Attorney General will still be required pursuant to Fed. R. Civ. P. 4(i)(1)(B).

(2) Where a complaint for administrative review is filed pursuant to 42 U.S.C. Section 405(g) and plaintiff is not proceeding in forma pauperis, service shall be accomplished pursuant to Fed. R. Civ. P. 4(I).

(D) Responsive Pleading, Transcript of Proceedings. The respondent has 120 days from the date of service of summons within which to file a responsive pleading and transcript of administrative proceedings.

(E) Motions: Hearing. Within 30 days after the filing of the responsive pleading and transcript, the plaintiff must file a Motion for Summary Judgment and a Memorandum of Law which must state with particularity which findings of the Commissioner are contrary to law. The plaintiff must identify the statute, regulation or case law under which the Commissioner allegedly erred. The plaintiff must cite to the record by page number the factual evidence which supports the plaintiff's position. Arguing generally, "the decision of the Commissioner is not supported by substantial evidence" is not sufficient to meet this rule. Within 45 days thereafter, the defendant must file a Cross–Motion and Memorandum of Law which must specifically respond to the plaintiff's assertions and arguments. The defendant must cite to the record by page number the factual evidence which supports the decision of the Commissioner. The case may be set for hearing at the discretion of the presiding judge.

[Effective January 20, 2010. Amended effective June 1, 2015.]

RULE 12.1 ANSWER TO PRISON-ER CIVIL RIGHTS CASES [DELETED EFFECTIVE JUNE 1, 2015]

RULE 40.1 ASSIGNMENT OF CASES AND PLACE OF FILING

(A) Peoria. All complaints and subsequent filings in cases which arise from the following counties: Fulton, Livingston, Marshall, McLean, Peoria, Putnam, Stark, Tazewell, and Woodford will be filed at PEORIA, ILLINOIS.

(B) Springfield. All complaints and subsequent filings in cases which arise from the following counties: Adams, Brown, Cass, Christian, DeWitt, Greene, Logan, Macoupin, Mason, Menard, Montgomery, Morgan, Pike, Sangamon, Scott, and Shelby, will be filed at SPRINGFIELD, ILLINOIS.

(C) Rock Island. All complaints and subsequent filings in cases which arise from the following counties: Bureau, Hancock, Henderson, Henry, Knox, McDonough, Mercer, Rock Island, Schuyler and Warren will be filed at ROCK ISLAND, ILLINOIS.

(D) Urbana. All complaints and subsequent filings in cases which arise from the following counties: Champaign, Coles, Douglas, Edgar, Ford, Iroquois, Kankakee, Macon, Moultrie, Piatt, and Vermillion will be filed at URBANA, ILLINOIS.

(E) All complaints and subsequent filings in cases filed in the Central District of Illinois must identify in the caption of such pleading or document, the division in which the case is pending.

(F) As part of the statement of jurisdiction, the initial pleadings in each case must state the basis for filing in the division selected.

[Effective January 20, 2010. Amended effective June 1, 2015.]

RULE 67.2 INVESTMENT OF REGISTRY FUNDS

(A) Unless a statute requires otherwise, funds shall be tendered to the Court or its officers for deposit into the registry only pursuant to court order. Unless provided for elsewhere in this rule, all money ordered to be paid into the Court or received by its officers in any case pending or adjudicated shall be deposited with the Treasurer of the United States in the name and to the credit of this Court pursuant to 28 U.S.C. § 2041 through depositaries designated by the Treasury to accept such deposit on its behalf.

(B) Unless otherwise ordered, all funds deposited into the registry shall be deposited in an interest bearing account through the Court Registry Investment System (CRIS) administered by the Administrative Office of the United States Courts.

(C) The custodian is authorized and directed by this rule to deduct, for maintaining accounts in CRIS, the registry fee. The proper registry fee is to be determined on the basis of the rates published by the Director of the Administrative Office of the United States Courts as approved by the Judicial Conference.

(D) Funds in the registry shall be disbursed only by court order. Before an order is entered directing the Clerk to release funds deposited in the registry of the court, the party must file a copy of such proposed order with the Financial Administrator. The order must specify the amount to be paid, the name of the person or persons to whom payment is to be made, and the name and address of the person or persons to whom the check is to be delivered.

[Effective January 20, 2010. Amended effective June 1, 2015.]

RULE 83.5 ADMISSION TO PRACTICE

(A) Qualifications for Admission to Practice. Any attorney licensed to·practice law in any state or in the District of Columbia must be admitted to practice generally in this court on written motion of a member in good standing of the bar of this court, or upon the attorney's own motion accompanied by certification of good standing from the state in which the attorney is licensed, and upon payment of the fees required by law and by Local Rule 83.5(E). On motion made at the time of the written motion for admission to practice, the presiding judge may waive the admission fees for any attorney employed full time by the United States, any state, or county.

Students of accredited law schools or law school graduates awaiting bar results may, upon written motion of a member in good standing of the bar of this court, be provisionally admitted to practice and may appear in this court under the supervision and direction of the sponsoring attorney. There will be no fee for provisional admission.

(B) Oath. All attorneys must, at the time of their admission to practice before this court, take an oath or affirmation to support the Constitution of the United States, faithfully to discharge their duties as attorneys and counselors, and to demean themselves uprightly and according to law and the recognized standards of ethics of the profession, and they must, under the direction of the clerk of this court, sign the oath of attorneys and pay the fees required by law and by Local Rule 83.5(E).

(C) Admission to Practice in All Divisions. Admission to practice generally in this court includes all divisions.

(D) Reciprocal Admission. Any attorney admitted to practice in District Courts of the Northern or Southern Districts of Illinois must be admitted to practice generally in this court upon the attorney's own motion accompanied by a copy of his/her admission certificate from the district in which the attorney is admitted, the attorney's certification that he/she is in good standing generally and upon payment of the fees required by law and Local Rule 83.5(E). Upon motion for reciprocal admission being allowed by the Court, movant will be summarily admitted to the CDIL bar.

(E) Fees Assessed Upon Admission. Each petitioner shall pay an admission fee upon the filing of the motion for admission, provided that in the event the petitioner is not admitted, the petitioner may request that the fee be refunded. The amount of the fee shall be established by the court, in conjunction with the fee prescribed by the Judicial Conference of the United States pursuant to 28 U.S.C. § 1914.

(F) Admission Pro Hac Vice. The court does not permit pro hac vice admissions generally. At the discretion of the presiding judge, an attorney who is duly licensed to practice in any state or the District of Columbia may file a motion seeking leave to participate in a case while his or her application for admission to prac-

tice in the Central District of Illinois is pending. The application for admission must be submitted contemporaneously with the motion for leave.

(G) Unauthorized Practice. All attorneys who appear in person or by filing pleadings in this court must be admitted to practice in this court in accordance with this Rule. Only attorneys so admitted may practice or file pleadings in this court. Except as provided in Local Rule 83.5(F), upon entry of appearance as an attorney of record, the entry of appearance must include a certification that the attorney is a member in good standing of the bar of this court.

Any person who, before his or her admission to the bar of this court, or during his or her suspension or disbarment, exercises in this district any of the privileges of a member of the bar in any action or proceedings pending in this court, or who pretends to be entitled to do so, may be adjudged guilty of contempt of court and appropriately sanctioned.

(H) Changes Reported to the Clerk of This Court. If at any time after admission any relevant circumstances change for an attorney (e.g., name, address, phone number, e-mail address, disciplinary status), he or she must notify the clerk of this court in writing of such change within 14 days.

(I) Admission. Admission shall be completed electronically unless otherwise allowed by the court. Procedures for admission will be prescribed by the clerk of this court. Admission is deemed to be as of the date the oath card is received by the clerk.

(J) Pro Bono Panel. The Pro Bono Panel of this court consists of all attorneys admitted to practice in this court whose place of business is in the Central District of Illinois. Attorneys employed full time by the United States, the State of Illinois or a county are exempt from service on the panel. Attorneys appointed pro bono to represent litigants may not enter into any contingent fee arrangement with their clients concerning the subject case. Statutory fees and expenses may be awarded to a pro bono attorney as provided by law.

Any attorney appointed to represent an indigent party in a civil proceeding before this Court may petition the Court for reimbursement of expenses incurred in preparation and presentation of the proceeding, subject to the procedures and regulations contained in the plan of this Court adopted June 1, 2000, governing reimbursement of expenses from the District Court Fund. [Effective January 20, 2010. Amended effective April 19, 2013; June 1, 2015.]

UNITED STATES BANKRUPTCY COURT FOR THE CENTRAL DISTRICT OF ILLINOIS

Including Amendments Received Through
August 1, 2015

MANUAL FOR PRACTITIONERS

ADRIENNE D. ATKINS, CLERK

Revised July 21, 2015

This Manual was prepared by
the deputy clerks of the U.S. Bankruptcy Court
for the Central District of Illinois
to assist those who practice here.

OFFICE OPERATIONS

	URBANA COURT	PEORIA COURT
Judge:	Mary P. Gorman, Chief Judge (Ch.7s & 11s) Thomas L. Perkins (Ch. 12 & 13s)	Thomas L. Perkins William V. Altenberger
Address:	203 United States Courthouse 201 South Vine Street, Urbana IL 61801	216 Federal Building 100 N.E. Monroe Street Peoria, IL 61602
Phone:	217/974–7330	309/671–7035
Office Hours:	Monday through Friday 8:00 a.m.–5:00 p.m.	Monday through Friday 8:00 a.m.–5:00 p.m.
Operations Manager:	Linda Blough	Michelle Heitzman

	SPRINGFIELD COURT	CLERK OF THE COURT
Judge:	Mary P. Gorman, Chief Judge	Adrienne D. Atkins
Address:	226 U.S. Courthouse 600 E. Monroe Street Springfield, IL 62701	226 U.S. Courthouse 600 E Monroe Street Springfield, IL 62701
Phone: Office Hours:	217/492–4551 Monday through Friday 8:00 a.m.—5:00 p.m.	Phone: 217/492–4551
Operations Manager:	Gerald Miller	Chief Deputy Clerk: Jeff Gustafson

McVCIS   Phone: 866–222–8029

SPECIAL NOTICES AND ALERTS

* Notice of an emergency or weather related closing of the Clerk's Office, including the cancellation or delay of court proceedings will appear at the court's website: www.ilcb. uscourts.gov
* A recorded voice message re: closing or delays will also be available by calling the main office phone numbers: Urbana 217–974–7330, Peoria 309–671–7035, Springfield 217–492–4551

* A broadcast email to all registered CM/ECF users will go out upon any emergency or weather related closing of the Clerk's Office.
* It is incumbent upon attorneys to check these sources and notify their clients accordingly.
* You should contact the Office of the US Trustee at 309–671–7854 regarding emergency or weather related cancellations of Meetings of Creditors.

BANKRUPTCY FEE SCHEDULE

The most current Bankruptcy Fee Schedule is located at www.ilcb.uscourts.gov under the Court Info tab.

LOCATIONS OF SECTION 341 MEETINGS

The County in which the petitioning debtor resides determines the location of the Section 341 Meeting.

URBANA DIVISION

Case numbers ___ -9 _____

County	Location of § 341 Meeting
Champaign	Urbana
Coles	Paris–Ch 7, Urbana –Ch. 13
Douglas	Paris–Ch. 7, Urbana—Ch. 13
Edgar	Paris–Ch. 7, Urbana–Ch. 13
Ford	Urbana
Iroquois	Kankakee
Kankakee	Kankakee
Livingston	Kankakee
Moultrie	Paris–Ch. 7, Urbana–Ch. 13
Piatt	Urbana
Vermilion	Urbana

Cases from the above counties are to be filed in Urbana, Illinois

Addresses of § 341 Meeting Locations:

Urbana
Urbana City Building
City Council Chambers
400 S. Vine Street
Urbana, IL 61801

Paris
Edgar County Courthouse
115 W. Court
Paris, IL 61944

Kankakee
Kankakee County Health Department
Conference Room
2390 W. Station Street
Kankakee, IL 60901

PEORIA DIVISION

Case numbers ____ -8 _____

County	Location of § 341 Meeting
Bureau	Peoria
Fulton	Peoria
Hancock	Galesburg
Henry	Rock Island
Knox	Galesburg
Marshall	Peoria
Peoria	Peoria
McDonough	Galesburg
Putnam	Peoria
Stark	Peoria
Tazewell	Peoria
Woodford	Peoria

Cases from the above counties are to be filed in Peoria, Illinois

County	Location of § 341 Meeting
Henderson	Galesburg
Mercer	Rock Island
Rock Island	Rock Island
Warren	Galesburg

Cases from the above counties may be filed in Peoria or Rock Island, Illinois

Addresses of § 341 Meeting Locations:

Peoria
1105 Becker Building
401 Main Street
Peoria, IL 61602

Rock Island
U.S. Post Office and Courthouse Building
211—19th Street
Courtroom 226
Rock Island, IL 61201

Galesburg—Chapter 7 only
Knox County Courthouse
200 S. Cherry Street
3rd Floor
Galesburg, IL 61401

Monmouth—Chapter 13 only
100 W. Broadway
Warren County Courthouse
3rd Floor, #A
Monmouth, IL 61462

SPRINGFIELD DIVISION

County	Location of § 341 Mtg.	County	Location of § 341 Mtg.	County	Location of § 341 Mtg.
Adams	Quincy	DeWitt:			
Brown	Quincy	Clinton	Decatur	Macon	Decatur
Cass	Springfield	DeWitt	Decatur	Macoupin	Springfield
Christian:		Farmer City	Bloomington	Mason	Springfield
Assumption	Decatur	Kenney	Decatur	McLean	Bloomington
Bulpitt	Springfield	Lane	Decatur	Menard	Springfield
Clarksdale	Springfield	Wapella	Bloomington	Montgomery	Springfield
Dunkel	Decatur	Waynesville	Bloomington	Morgan	Springfield
Edinburg	Springfield	Weldon	Decatur	Pike	Quincy
Hewittsville	Springfield	Greene	Springfield	Sangamon	Springfield
Jeiseyville	Springfield	Logan:		Schuyler	Quincy
Kincaid	Springfield	Atlanta	Bloomington	Scott	Quincy
Langleyville	Springfield	Beason	Decatur	Shelby	Decatur
Millersville	Springfield	Broadwell	Springfield		
Morrisonville	Springfield	Chestnut	Decatur		
Mt. Auburn	Decatur	Cornland	Springfield		
Owaneco	Springfield	Elkhart	Springfield		
Palmer	Springfield	Emden	Springfield		
Pana	Springfield	Hartsburg	Bloomington		
Rosamond	Springfield	Lake Fork	Decatur		
Sharpsburg	Springfield	Latham	Decatur		
Stonington	Springfield	Lawndale	Bloomington		
Taylorville	Springfield	Lincoln	Springfield		
Tovey	Springfield	Middletown	Springfield		
Willeys	Springfield	Mt. Pulaski	Decatur		
		New Holland	Springfield		
		San Jose	Bloomington		

Cases from the above counties are to be filed in Springfield, Illinois

Addresses of § 341 meeting Locations:

Bloomington

Chapter 7, 12:	Law and Justice Center Courtroom 3E 104 W. Front Bloomington, IL 61701	
Chapter 13:	Law and Justice Center Courtroom 5B, 5th Floor 104 W. Front Bloomington, IL 61701	
Chapter 11:	Law and Justice Center Operations Room 104 W. Front Bloomington, IL 61701	

Decatur

Chapter 7, 11, 12, 13:	Macon County Courthouse Courtroom 5C 253 E. Wood St. Decatur, IL 62523

Quincy

Chapter 7, 11,12:	Courtroom 2D Adams County Courthouse 521 Vermont Quincy, IL 62301
Chapter 13:	Adams County Courthouse 2nd Floor, Small Jury Room 521 Vermont Quincy, IL 62301

Springfield

Chapter 7, 11, 12, 13:	Illinois Building 607 E. Adams Street 1st Floor Springfield, IL 62701

CENTRAL DISTRICT OF ILLINOIS TRUSTEES

CHAPTER 7   Charles Covey, 700 Commerce Bank Building, Peoria, IL 61602
(309) 673–3807

A. Clay Cox, P.O. Box 3067, Bloomington, IL 61702–3067
(309) 828–7331

James R. Inghram, Bank of America Bldg., 529 Hampshire Street, Suite 409, Quincy, IL 62301
(217) 222–7420

Mariann Pogge, 3300 Hedley Road, Springfield, IL 62711
(217) 793–7412

Roger L. Prillaman, 220 West Main Street, Urbana, IL 61801
(217) 384-1300

Gary Rafool, 411 Hamilton Boulevard #1600, Peoria, IL 61602
(309) 673-5535

Jeana K. Reinbold, P.O. Box 7315, Springfield, IL 62791
(217) 801-4090

Jeffrey D. Richardson, 132 S. Water St., Suite 444, Decatur, IL
62523
(217) 425-1515

John L. Swartz, 1 W. Old State Capitol Plz, #600, P.O. Box 2117,
Springfield, IL 62705
(217) 525-1571

Kristin L. Wilson, P.O. Box 137, 611 6th Street,
Charleston, IL 61920
(217) 345-3079

Pamela S. Wilcox, P.O. Box 1806, Galesburg, IL 61402
(309) 341-6036

CHAPTER 12   Michael Clark, 401 Main Street, Ste. 1130, Peoria, IL 61602-1241
(309) 674-6137

CHAPTER 13   Marsha L. Combs–Skinner, 108 S. Broadway, Newman, IL 61942
(217) 837-9730

Michael Clark, 401 Main Street, Ste. 1130, Peoria, IL 61602-1241
(309) 674-6137

John H. Germeraad, P.O. Box 9768,
Springfield, IL 62791 (217) 670-1741

UNITED STATES TRUSTEE

Nancy J. Gargula
United States Trustee
Becker Building, Room 1100
401 Main
Peoria, IL 61602
(309) 671-7854

COMMONLY USED FEDERAL AND STATE AGENCY ADDRESSES

For all Chapters

Internal Revenue Service
P.O. Box 7346
Philadelphia, PA 19101-7346

When scheduling Veterans
Administration as a creditor,
if no other address available use

Veterans Administration
Regional Office
POB 8136
536 S. Clark
Chicago, IL 60680

When scheduling Farmers Home
Administration, Dept. of
Agriculture, ASCS—Farmers Home

Farmers Home Administration
U.S. Dept. of Agriculture
Illini Plaza, Suite 103

Administration, use as an additional address	1817 S. Neil St. Champaign IL 61820
When scheduling Dept. of Agriculture, ASCS—Farmers Home Administration, ASCS, Commodity Credit Corp., use as an additional address	**USDA—IL State ASCS Office** 2305 W. Monroe St., #1 POB 19273 Springfield, IL 62794
When scheduling Federal Crop Insurance Corp., use as an additional address	**USDA—IL State ASCS Office** 2305 W. Monroe St., #2 Springfield, IL 62794
When scheduling Federal Housing Administration, use as an additional address	**Federal Housing Administration** Dept. of Housing & Urban Development Washington, D.C. 20411
When scheduling State of IL for taxes (R.O.T., Sales tax, Withholding tax, Income Tax, or if tax not designated)	**IL Dept. of Revenue** Bankruptcy Section P.O. Box 64338 Chicago, IL 60664–0338
When scheduling State of IL for unemployment taxes, payroll	**IL Dept. of Employment Security** Insolvency/Bkcy Subunit Field Audit Section 33 S. State St. Chicago, IL 60603 also add: **Attorney General** 33 S. State St. Room 992 Chicago, IL 60603
When scheduling State of IL for franchise tax	**State of IL** Corporation Dept. Franchise Tax Div. Springfield, IL 62706
When scheduling Dept. of Public Aid	**IL Dept. of Public Aid** Bureau of Collections Jesse B. Harris Bldg. 100 S. Grand Ave. East Springfield, IL 62762
When scheduling State of IL student loan	**IL State Scholarship Commission** 1755 Lake Cook Rd. Deerfield, IL 60015
When scheduling real estate and personal property taxes	**County Collector** —————— County ——————, IL (zip code)
When debtor engaged in business of transporting persons or property, use as an additional address	**Chief Counsel** Transportation Audits GSA—General Law Division Room 4124 Washington, D.C. 20405
When debtor is a land developer, use as an additional address	**Dept. of Housing & Urban Development** Office of Interstate Land Sales Registration Washington, D.C. 20410
When scheduling a component of U.S. Army, use as an additional address	**Commander** U.S. Army Finance & Acctg Center

Attn: FINCL
Indianapolis, IN 46249

When scheduling a component of U.S.
Navy, use as an additional address

Department of Navy
Navy Finance Center
Federal Bldg.
Cleveland, OH 44199

When scheduling Economic Development
Administration (Economic Development
Administration, U.S. Dept. of
Commerce, EDA), use as an additional
address

**Ass't Chief Counsel for Litigation and
Liquidation**
Economic Development Administration
Room 7106
U.S. Dept. of Commerce
Washington, D.C. 20230

When scheduling U.S. Postal Service,
use as an additional address

Postmaster General
U.S. Postal Service
475 L'Enfant Plaza
Washington, D.C. 20260

When scheduling a debt to the United
States other than for taxes BR
2002(j)

Name of Agency
c/o U.S. Attorney
318 South Sixth Street
Springfield, IL 62701–1626

SEARCH FEE GUIDELINES

You are encouraged to call the free computer line (VCIS), use PACER, or obtain free information in person with the use of Computer Terminals in each staffed office.

ALL REQUESTS MUST BE IN WRITING or IN PERSON
NO INFORMATION WILL BE GIVEN BY PHONE

SEARCH FEE OF $30.00 (paid in advance)

Any request requiring a physical search of court records in computer or in the case file by Deputy Clerk is considered a Search of Record and requires a $30.00 fee plus $ .50 per page of copywork paid in advance for:

All written requests; (See exceptions under "No Search Fee")

Information whether an entity is listed as a creditor;

Copies of petition, schedules, and other documents;

All in-person requests if Deputy Clerk must search the file for information. *No search fee if deputy retrieves file for person to view or if documents to be copied have been marked with paper clips by requesting party.*

No Search Fee to Obtain:

Case Number when exact name of debtor is provided;

Date bankruptcy filed when exact name of debtor is provided;

Name of debtor when case number is provided;

Social Security number of debtor;

Whether case was filed as a voluntary case or an involuntary case;

Chapter Number of originally filed case;

Name of Debtor's Attorney;

Name of Trustee;

Whether the case is an Asset Case or a No Asset Case;

Date No Asset Report filed;

Date Final Report filed;

Date Discharge issued;

Date, Time and Place of Sec. 341 Meeting;

General Status of Case—Pending or Closed;

Date Notice of Appeal filed, if applicable.

COPYWORK POLICY

There are several ways to obtain copies of documents:

Print Electronic Records from your Personal Computer using PACER

You may print copies of documents, download documents to your own computer or search information in your case. The PACER system is available days, nights and weekends.

You must register to become a user at the PACER website (http://www.pacer.gov). There is a fee for copies of $.10 per page. A user is not billed until charges of $15 in a quarter have accrued. Most one-time users would not accrue enough charges to be billed for copies. You will find a full explanation of charges on the PACER website as well as directions for registration

Print Electronic Records at the Clerk's Office from Public Computer Terminals

You can print electronic records form the PACER (Public Access to Court Electronic Records) computer terminals located in each of our three offices. You will be charged $.10 cents per page. Please note, the Clerk's Office can only accept EXACT CHANGE and cannot make or give change.

Submit a Written Request by Email or Mail

You may send a written request for copies by email or mail to the office where your case was filed:

Copywork_Urb@ilcb.uscourts.gov

Copywork_Peo@ilcb.uscourts.gov

Copywork_Spr@ilcb.uscourts.gov

Your request must include:

Your name

The case number or name of debtor(s)

A description of the copies requested or document numbers

Once we receive your request, we will send you a statement of charges for the copywork. You will be charged $.50 per page for copies. If your request requires a search of the records, a $30.00 search fee is required.

After you receive the statement of charges, mail payment to the Clerk's Office via money order, cashier check, or company/firm check made payable to: Clerk, U.S. Bankruptcy Court. The Clerk's Office does not accept personal checks or cash through the mail.

After we receive payment, copies will be made and sent to you via email or first class mail. Please specify how you would like copies returned to you and provide the necessary information to do so. Please note: If you choose to have copies returned to you by email, your receipt will be sent by email as well.

ARCHIVED CASES

Cases closed prior to 2004 are stored in the Federal Records Center (FRC) in Chicago and copies may be obtained directly from the FRC. Contact the Clerk's Office to obtain location information.

PAYMENT BY CHECK OR CASH

Submit Money Order, Certified Check, Bank Cashier Check, or Business Check ONLY.

CHECKS:

Make payable to: Clerk, U.S. Bankruptcy Court

or

                      U.S. Bankruptcy Court

NOT ACCEPTED:

Personal Check

Third Party Check

Blank Check

Unsigned Check

Incorrect Amount—amount must be **EXACT**

Numerical Figure and Written Amount do not agree

Postdated Check

Check made payable to an unacceptable party—*See above*

NOTE**—*There is a $53.00 service charge on all returned checks.*

CASH:

No Foreign Money accepted.

Must be **EXACT AMOUNT** only. We do not make change.

Cash payments accepted only in person at the counter.

Cash received in mail will be promptly returned.

INFORMATION ON ORDERING A TRANSCRIPT

Springfield Office

Requests for transcripts of proceedings held after 2/2007 must be submitted on the Transcript Order Form at http://www.uscourts.gov/uscourts/FormsAndFees/Forms/AO435. pdf. Please complete items 1–19 and return the form to the Bankruptcy Clerk's Office. Upon receipt of the completed form, you will be notified of the cost for the transcript. PREPAYMENT IS REQUIRED BEFORE ANY ORDER WILL BE PROCESSED.

Requests for transcripts of proceedings held between 11/2000 and 2/2007 must be sent directly to:

Carla Boehl
17804 Edwards Rd
Virden, IL 62690
217–965–3006

Please contact the Bankruptcy Clerk's Office at 217–492–4551 if you have questions regarding the procedures for ordering a transcript.

Peoria Office

Requests for transcripts must be submitted on the Transcript Order Form at http://www. uscourts.gov/uscourts/FormsAndFees/Forms/AO435.pdf. Please complete items 1–19 and return the form to the Bankruptcy Clerk's Office. Upon receipt of the completed form, you will be notified of the cost for the transcript. PREPAYMENT IS REQUIRED BEFORE ANY ORDER WILL BE PROCESSED.

Tape recordings of certain judicial hearings may be ordered by submitting your request in writing to the Bankruptcy Clerk's Office. You will then be notified of the total cost ($30.00 per tape). The Bankruptcy Clerk's Office does not transcribe tapes.

Please contact the Bankruptcy Clerk's Office at 309–671–7035 if you have questions regarding the procedures for ordering a transcript.

Urbana Office

Requests for transcripts of proceedings held after 4/18/95 must be submitted on the Transcript Order Form at http://www.uscourts.gov/uscourts/FormsAndFees/Forms/AO435.pdf. Please complete items 1–19 and return the form to the Bankruptcy Clerk's Office. Upon receipt of the completed form, you will be notified of the cost for the transcript. PREPAYMENT IS REQUIRED BEFORE ANY ORDER WILL BE PROCESSED.

Tape recordings of certain judicial hearings may be ordered by submitting your request in writing to the Bankruptcy Clerk's Office. You will then be notified of the total cost ($30.00 per tape). The Bankruptcy Clerk's Office does not transcribe tapes.

Requests for transcripts of proceedings held prior to 4/18/95 must sent directly to the Court Reporter as indicated below:

For proceedings held in Urbana or Paris	For proceedings held in Kankakee
Maninfior Court Reporting	Contact the Clerk's Office in
PO Box 1036	Urbana
Mattoon, IL 61938	
217–235–1127	

Please contact the Bankruptcy Clerk's Office, 217–974–7330, if you have questions regarding the procedures for ordering transcripts or tapes.

PACER

(Public Access to Court Electronic Records)

Web Version

Introduction

PACER is available on the Internet in a web-based format.

Note: Each court controls its own computer system and case information database; therefore, there will be some variations among jurisdictions as to the information offered.

Persons interested in utilizing this service must first register with the PACER Service Center at 800 676–6856. The website for the PACER Service Center is: http://pacer.uscourts.gov/

There is a charge of $.10/page for information retrieved from this site. A user is not billed until charges of $15 in a quarterly billing cycle have accrued. **Most *one-time users* would not accrue enough charges to be billed for copies.** You will find a full explanation of charges on the PACER website as well as directions for registration.

For more information: http://www.ilcb.uscourts.gov/obtaining-copies-documents-bankruptcy-case-file

REGISTRY OF MAILING ADDRESSES FOR STATE & GOVERNMENTAL UNITS

* **Illinois Attorney General**
 33 S. State Street, Room 993
 Chicago, IL 60603

* **Illinois Attorney General**
 Revenue Litigation 500 S.
 Second Street Springfield,
 IL 62701

* **U.S. Attorney General**
 U.S. Department of Justice 950
 Pennslyvania Avenue, NW
 Washington, DC 20530–0001

*** Treasurer of the State of Illinois**
 Office of the State Treasurer Legal
 Department
 James R. Thompson Center 100 W.
 Randolph Street Suite 15–600
 Chicago, Illinois 60601

* **U.S. Securities and Exchange Commission**
 175 W. Jackson Blvd., Suite 900
 Chicago, IL 60604

* **Illinois Department of Revenue**
 Bankruptcy Section
 P.O. Box 64338 Chicago, IL

* **U.S. Attorney**
  318 South Sixth Street
  Springfield, IL 62701

*Illinois Capital Development Board
  Chief Counsel
  401 S. Spring St., 3rd Floor
  Springfield, Illinois 62706

*Illinois Department of Human Services
  General Counsel
  100 W. Randolph, Suite 6–400
  Chicago, Illinois 60601

*Illinois Department of Natural Resources
  Chief Legal Counsel
  1 Natural Resources Way
  Springfield, Illinois 62703

*Illinois Department of Public Aid
  William C. Kurylak
  Office of General Counsel
  401 South Clinton Street, 6th Floor
  Chicago, Illinois 60607

*Illinois Department of Public Health
  Division of Legal Services Attn:
  Bankruptcy Notice 535 West
  Jefferson, 5th Floor Springfield,
  Illinois 62761

*Texas Workforce Commission
  Bankruptcy Unit, Rm 556 101
  E. 15th St.
  Austin, TX 78778–0001

*Illinois Department of Employment Security
  Insolvency/Bkcy Subunit Field
  Audit Section
  33 S. State St. 10th Floor
  Chicago, IL 60603

60664–0338

* **Internal Revenue Service**
  P.O. Box 7346 Philadelphia, PA
  19101–7346

*Mississippi State Tax Commission
  Bankruptcy Section
  P.O. Box 22808 Jackson, MS
  39225–2808

*U.S. Environmental Protection Agency
  Richard L. Nagle
  Bankruptcy Contact
  US EPA Region 5 Mail Code: C–14J 77 W.
  Jackson Blvd.
  Chicago, IL 60604

*California Franchise Tax Board
  Service of Adversary Proceedings: Chief
  Counsel
  Franchise Tax Board
  c/o General Counsel Section
  P.O. Box 1720, MS: A–260 Rancho Cordova,
  CA 95741–1720

  Bankruptcy Code § 505 Requests:
  Franchise Tax Board
  Bankruptcy Section, MS: A–340
  PO Box 2952
  Sacramento, CA 95812–2952

  All Other Service and Notices:
  Franchise Tax Board Bankruptcy
  Section, MS: A–340 P.O. Box 2952
  Sacramento, CA 95812–2952

  11 U.S.C. § 505(b) Requests
  Michigan Department of Treasury, Tax Policy Division
  ATTN:
  Litigation Liaison
  2nd Floor, Austin Building
  430 West Allegan Street
  Lansing, Michigan 48922

  Oklahoma Tax Commission
  Office of the General Counsel, Bankruptcy Section
  120 N. Robinson, Ste. 2000W
  Oklahoma City, OK 73102

McVCIS

(Multi–Court Voice Case Information System)

INTRODUCTION

McVCIS is a service provided by the federal bankruptcy courts which allows you to get information about any pending bankruptcy case filed in the Central District of Illinois by using a standard touch tone telephone. McVCIS, also allows you to search for case information in numerous other federal bankruptcy courts.

I. McVCIS

By dialing toll free 866–222–8029 from a touchtone phone, you may determine whether a party has filed for bankruptcy, and gain a considerable amount of case information. The service is available at all times. The information available includes debtor(s)' name(s), date of filing, chapter, attorney for the debtor, trustee (if any), date and time of the pending Sec. 341 Meeting, date of discharge, date of case closing, and general case status, such as "Awaiting 341 Meeting" or "Awaiting Discharge Order." Simply enter the debtor's name, last name first, using up to ten characters, and hit the # sign. Punctuation is irrelevant, and we recommend that you use all 10 characters allotted. If the debtor is a corporation, enter the first ten characters of the debtor's name and hit the # sign.

EQUIPMENT NEEDED

A touch-tone telephone

HOURS

The system is available 24 hours every day.

HOW TO USE McVCIS

To use McVCIS, simply follow these instructions:

1. For cases filed January 1, 2004 through current date—Dial 866–222–8029.

2. For most cases closed prior to January 1, 2004, contact the Clerk's Office for help.

3. When prompted to enter the state and division, say "Illinois Central"

4. Press 1 for instructions on how to use this system or say "help", press 2 to search by case number or say "case number", press 3 to search by participant's name or same "name", press 4 to search by participant's social security or say "social security number".

GENERAL INFORMATION

LOCAL RULES

There are no local rules in the Central District of Illinois Bankruptcy Court. The local rules of the U.S. District Court for the Central District of Illinois and the Federal Rules of Bankruptcy Procedure apply. The local District Court rules can be found at http://www.ilcd.uscourts.gov/. District Court's local rules may also be obtained in person at one of the District Clerk's Offices or by submitting a stamped, self addressed 9½″ × 12″ envelope with $4.95 postage prepaid to U.S. District Court, 151 U.S. Courthouse, 600 E. Monroe Street, Springfield, Illinois 62701.

INSTRUCTION PAMPHLETS AVAILABLE

There are pamphlets available in each of the divisional offices which briefly outline the basic information, filing requirements, and guidelines for preparing the creditor matrix for Chapter 7 and Chapter 13 bankruptcies.

EMERGENCY FILINGS

For emergency filings when the Clerk's Office is not open, contact the Clerk of Court, Adrienne D. Atkins at 217–720–1881.

SETTING MATTERS FOR HEARING

The Clerk's Office will set matters for hearing on the first available court date. There is no need to formally request a hearing.

DISCHARGE ORDERS

Unless an objection has been filed, discharge orders will be mailed approximately eight weeks from the date the first meeting of creditors was originally set.

AMENDMENTS

When submitting amendments to the matrix, lists or schedules D, E, or F, please submit only the changes.

BANKRUPTCY NOTICING CENTERS AND UNDELIVERABLE MAIL

Many of our notices including 341 Notices and Discharges are now produced and mailed from the Bankruptcy Noticing Centers in Virginia and Utah. For this reason, the documents are being received several days later than the ones which are mailed locally. It is the responsibility of the Attorney for the Debtor to readdress and re-send undeliverable mail and then notify the Court as to any changes of address.

UPDATE YOUR EMAIL ADDRESS

CM/ECF Users are required to maintain and update their personal information, including email addresses. Failure to maintain a current email address may result in the lockout of your CM/ECF filing account. See Maintain User Information for instructions.

CM/ECF INFORMATION AND TIPS

Click the "ECF Helpdesk" tab from the court's website http://www.ilcb.uscourts.gov

DEBTOR ELECTRONIC BANKRUPTCY NOTICING (DeBN)

Note: Only the court is authorized to send notices to the debtor through this DeBN program. All other parties, such as trustees and creditors, will continue to serve the debtor via U.S. mail or in person as required by court rules.

The U.S. Bankruptcy Court for the Central District of Illinois now offers debtors the opportunity to request receipt of court notices and orders via email, instead of U.S. mail, through a program called "Debtor Electronic Bankruptcy Noticing" or "DeBN."

DeBN provides the following advantages:

- **Faster**—You'll receive notices the same day they are filed by the court.
- **Convenient**—Access your notices anywhere you have internet access.
- **No more lost paperwork**—Storing notices on your computer means never losing a paper copy.
- **Less paper clutter**—Helps the environment and reduces paper clutter in your home.
- **It is FREE!**

Pursuant to Federal Rule of Bankruptcy Procedure 9036, a party may make a written request for delivery of notices via email, instead of U.S. mail. Through the DeBN program, only notices and orders that have been filed by the court can be emailed to the debtor. Debtors requesting participation in the DeBN program must complete and file a Debtor's Electronic Noticing Request (DeBN) form with the court where their case is filed.

Go to www.ilcb.uscourts.gov/debn for more information and to download the request form.

[Effective March 13, 2012. Amended effective April 4, 2013; February 7, 2014; March 23, 2015; July 21, 2015.]

UNITED STATES BANKRUPTCY COURT FOR THE SOUTHERN DISTRICT OF ILLINOIS

Including Amendments Received Through
August 1, 2015

ORDERS

GENERAL ORDER 15–1. IN RE: ATTORNEY'S FEES IN CHAPTER 13 SIGNATURE ON CHAPTER 13 PLAN

ORDER

The Court hereby ORDERS as follows:

1. Effective immediately, the amount of fees paid to debtor's counsel pre-confirmation is increased to $2,500.00 (inclusive of funds received pre–petition). This Order applies to all active cases. The chapter 13 trustees shall have thirty (30) days in which to make the change to existing, unconfirmed cases. The total flat fee shall remain at $4,000.00 for consumer cases and $4,500.00 for business cases.

2. Effective immediately, the requirement in the Chapter 13 Procedures Manual limiting attorney fees to $1,500.00 for cases that convert to chapter 7 pre-confirmation is stricken.

3. Effective immediately, upon conversion of a chapter 13 case to chapter 7, the chapter 13 trustee shall file with the Court a "Statement of Attorney's Fees Disbursed by the Chapter 13 Trustee."

4. Effective January 1, 2017, the pre-confirmation amount paid to debtor's counsel shall increase to $2,750.00, and the total flat fee shall increase to $4,500.00 for consumer cases and $5,000.00 for business cases.

5. Effective immediately, if debtor is represented by counsel, the debtor's signature is not required on chapter 13 plans filed with the Court. Counsel shall maintain some type of verification from debtor indicating the debtor's knowledge and approval of the plan as filed. Failure to do so will result in the imposition of sanctions by the Court, including but not limited to disgorgement of attorney fees.

A revised Chapter 13 Procedures Manual reflecting the above changes, as well as a revised form plan (with a new signature page) will be posted on the Court's website.

[Dated: July 21, 2015.]

CHAPTER 13 PROCEEDINGS—SELECTED FORMS

REVISED UNIFORM CHAPTER 13 PLAN

UNITED STATES BANKRUPTCY COURT
SOUTHERN DISTRICT OF ILLINOIS

In re:	)	Case No.
	)	☐ Original Chapter 13 Plan
	)	☐ Amended Plan Number _____
	)	(Changes must be underlined)
Debtor(s)	)	☐ Limited Service Applicable

CHAPTER 13 PLAN AND NOTICE OF TIME TO OBJECT

CHAPTER 13 PROCEDURES MANUAL. The provisions of the Court's Chapter 13 Procedures Manual are incorporated herein by reference and made part of this Plan. This manual is available at *www.ilsb.uscourts.gov.*

YOUR RIGHTS WILL BE AFFECTED. You should read these papers carefully and discuss them with your attorney. Anyone opposing any provision of this Plan as set forth below must file a timely written objection. This Plan may be confirmed without further notice or hearing unless written objection is filed and served within 21 days after the conclusion of the 11 U.S.C. § 341(a) Meeting of Creditors. Objections to an amended Plan must be filed and served within 21 days after the date of filing of the amended Plan.

If you have a secured claim, this Plan may void or modify your lien if you do not object to the Plan.

THIS PLAN DOES NOT ALLOW CLAIMS. A Creditor must file a timely Proof of Claim to receive distribution as set forth in this Plan. Even if the Plan provides for payment, no payment will be made unless a Proof of Claim is timely filed.

1. PAYMENTS

The Debtor submits to the Standing Chapter 13 Trustee all projected disposable income to be received within the applicable commitment period of the Plan. The payment schedule is as follows:

Start Month#	End Month #	Monthly Payment	Total

Total Months: _____   Grand Total Payments: _____

Wage Order Required: ☐ Yes ☐ No **The Debtor from whose check the payment is deducted:** _____

Employer's name, address, city, state, phone: _____

_____

☐ This Plan cures any previous arrearage in payments to the Chapter 13 Trustee under any prior Plan filed in this case.

IMPORTANT PAYMENT INFORMATION

NOTE: Plan payments to the Trustee must commence within 30 days of the filing of the petition. The Debtor must make direct payments to the Trustee by money order or cashier's check until the employer deduction begins. Include your name and case number on your money order or cashier's check. Contact the Trustee for the payment mailing address.

ORDER OF DISTRIBUTION

The following order of priority shall be utilized with respect to all payments received under the Plan terms:

1. Any unpaid portion of the filing fee;

2. Notice fees equal to $.50 per page of the Plan, multiplied by the number of creditors listed on the debtor's schedules;

3. The Trustee's fees for each disbursement, the percentage of which is fixed by the U.S. Trustee;

4. Ongoing mortgage payments on real estate;

5. Allowed administrative expenses;

6. Attorney's fees and other secured creditors as set forth in the Chapter 13 Procedures Manual;

7. Priority creditors as set forth in the Plan;

8. Any special class of unsecured creditors as set forth in the Plan; and

9. General unsecured creditors.

2. *ADMINISTRATIVE EXPENSES*

Administrative Creditor	Estimated Amount of Claim

ATTORNEY'S FEES

Attorney name: _____

☐ Flat fee through Plan $ _____ **OR**

☐ The Debtor's counsel elects to be paid on an hourly basis and will file a fee application(s) for approval of fees. No fees shall be disbursed until a fee application is approved by the Court. However, the Trustee shall reserve a total of $4,000.00 for payment toward such application, pursuant to the Order of Distribution and the Chapter 13 Procedures Manual.

3. *REAL ESTATE—CURING DEFAULTS AND MAINTAINING PAYMENTS*

Post-petition payments shall be made by the Trustee if (i) a pre-petition default exists; (ii) a post-petition, pre-confirmation default occurs; or (iii) a post-confirmation default arises that cannot be cured by the Debtor within six months. Otherwise, post-petition payments may be made directly by the Debtor to the creditor. Where the Trustee is disbursing the ongoing payments, the first mortgage payment to be disbursed will be that which becomes due in the second month after the month in which the petition is filed. In this situation, a mortgage holder should file a "pre-petition" claim that includes both the pre-petition arrearage and all post-petition contractual payments not disbursed by the Trustee as set forth above. Similarly, a Debtor must include the amount of any such payment(s) in the pre-petition arrearage calculation. (See the Chapter 13 Procedures Manual for examples and further instruction.)

For ongoing payments brought in due to a post-petition default, payments by the Trustee are to begin on the first due date after the month in which the amended or modified Plan is filed, or as otherwise ordered by the Court. All payments received from the Trustee must be credited by the creditor as the Plan directs. Pursuant to 11 U.S.C. § 524(i), ongoing post-petition mortgage payments tendered under the Plan by either the Trustee or the Debtor shall be credited by the holder and/or servicer of said claim only to such payments and may not be used for any other purpose without prior approval of the Court. Pursuant to 11 U.S.C. § 524(i), payments for pre-petition mortgage arrearages tendered under the Plan by the Trustee shall be credited by the holder and/or servicer of said claim only to such arrearages and may not be used for any other purpose without prior Court approval.

The Chapter 13 Procedures Manual sets forth the terms concerning notice of payment changes; notice of fees, expenses and charges; form and content of said notice; determination of fees, expenses or charges; notice of final cure payment; response to notice of final cure payment; determination of final cure and payment; and the consequences of the failure to notify. If a conflict arises between the terms set forth in the Chapter 13 Procedures Manual and any bankruptcy rule, the federal and local bankruptcy rule(s) shall supercede the Manual.

A) Payment of ongoing post-petition mortgage payments by the Debtor is as follows:

Creditor	Estimated Month-ly Payment	Payment Start Date	Payment End Date

B) Payment of ongoing post-petition mortgage payments by the Trustee is as follows:

Creditor	Payment Address	Estimated Monthly Pay-ment	Payment Start Date	Payment End Date

The estimated monthly payment amount referenced in Part 3A and 3B above may change based upon Proof(s) of Claim filed and/or subsequent Supplemental Proof(s) of Claim.

C) Payment of pre and/or post-petition arrearages, arising from a default in mortgage payments that were being made directly by the Debtor to the creditor, is as follows:

Creditor	Property Address	Lien No.	Estimated Amount of Claim

D) Payment of post-petition arrearages, arising from a default in Plan payments, is as follows:

Creditor	Total Amount of Post-petition Claim

Use of this section is more fully explained in the Chapter 13 Procedures Manual. In summary, this section should be used (i) when the ongoing mortgage payment is being disbursed by the Chapter 13 Trustee and (ii) the post-petition arrearage arises from a default by the Debtor in the Plan payments. Furthermore, the use of this section constitutes an affirmative representation by the filing party that the Debtor and creditor(s) have agreed to have this post-petition arrearage paid as a separate claim *unless the next box is checked.*

☐ By checking this box, the filing party represents that he or she has made reasonable and diligent efforts to secure an agreement with the creditor for the above-described treatment of this post-petition arrearage. Furthermore, upon request by any party in interest, the filing party shall provide a detailed, written explanation of the steps taken to attempt to secure an agreement with the creditor. Abuse of the letter and spirit of this provision may subject the filing party to any sanctions the Court deems appropriate.

If attorney's fees are to be sought in conjunction with this post-petition arrearage, a Proof of Claim for said fees must be filed with the Court and a separate agreed order submitted to the Court.

E) Real Estate Property Tax Claims shall be paid as follows: To the extent that taxes are due or will become due, they will be paid directly by the Debtor or pursuant to any applicable note and mortgage on the property.

F) Real Estate Secured Claims to which 11 U.S.C. § 506 Valuation is Applicable ("Cram Down Claims"):
Claims listed in this subsection are debts secured by real estate that is not the Debtor's primary residence. These claims will be paid either the value of the secured property as stated below or the secured amount of that claim as listed on the Proof of Claim, whichever is less, with interest as provided below. Any portion of a claim that exceeds the value of the secured property will be treated as an unsecured claim without the necessity of an objection.

Creditor/Collateral	Value	Estimated Claim	Interest Rate	Estimated Monthly Payment
			0.00%	
			0.00%	
			0.00%	

4. *SECURED CLAIMS AND VALUATION OF COLLATERAL UNDER 11 U.S.C. SECTION 506*

A) Secured Claims to which 11 U.S.C. § 506 Valuation is NOT Applicable ("910 Claims"):
Claims listed in this subsection are debts secured by a purchase-money security interest in a personal motor vehicle acquired for the personal use of the debtor, incurred within the 910 days preceding the date of the filing of the bankruptcy *or* debts secured by a purchase-money security interest in "any other thing of value" incurred within one year preceding the date of the filing of the bankruptcy. *These claims will be paid in full with interest as provided below.*

Creditor/Collateral	Estimated Claim	Interest Rate	Estimated Monthly Payment
		0.00%	
		0.00%	
		0.00%	

B) Secured Claims to which 11 U.S.C. § 506 Valuation is Applicable ("Cram Down Claims"):
Claims listed in this subsection are debts secured by personal property *not* described in the immediately preceding paragraph of this Plan. These claims will be paid either the value of the secured property as stated below or the secured amount of that claim as listed on the Proof of Claim, whichever is less, with interest as provided below. Any portion of a claim that exceeds the value of the secured property will be treated as an unsecured claim without the necessity of an objection.

Creditor/Collateral	Value	Estimated Claim	Interest Rate	Estimated Monthly Payment
			0.00%	
			0.00%	
			0.00%	

C) Surrender of Property:
This section allows for the surrender of collateral. The Debtor surrenders any and all right, title and interest in the following collateral. If the creditor believes that it may be entitled to a deficiency claim under applicable law, then the secured creditor must file its secured claim before the non-governmental claims bar date. Within 90 days following the claims bar date, the secured creditor shall file an amended Proof of Claim indicating the unsecured deficiency balance (if any), unless an extension is approved by the Court. Any objection to a timely filed

deficiency claim shall be filed within 45 days of the date the deficiency claim was filed, or the same is deemed allowed. Absent leave of Court, deficiency claims filed outside of this 90–day period (or any extension granted by the Court) are deemed disallowed without action by any party. Upon entry of the Order lifting the automatic stay, the Debtor must reasonably cooperate with the creditor in either making the collateral available for pickup or in supplying information of the collateral's last known location.

Creditor	Collateral Surrendered	Estimated Monies Previously Paid by the Trustee

5. *SEPARATELY CLASSIFIED CLAIMS*

Creditor	Secured/ Unsecured	Estimated Claim	Interest Rate	Paid By
			0.00%	
			0.00%	
			0.00%	

6. *EXECUTORY CONTRACTS AND UNEXPIRED LEASES*

All executory contracts and unexpired leases are *rejected*, except the following which are assumed:

A) Payment of executory contracts and unexpired leases *directly* by the Debtor is as follows:

Creditor	Collateral	Monthly Payment	# of Payments Remaining

B) Payment of arrearages by the Trustee is as follows:

Creditor	Collateral	Address	Est. Claim	Int. Rate	Estimated Monthly Payment
				0.00%	
				0.00%	
				0.00%	

Since the claims in Part 3F, 4A, 4B and 6B are based on the allowed claim amount, the estimated monthly payment in those sections is provided by the Debtor for reference only.

7. *PRIORITY CLAIMS*

A) Domestic Support Obligations:

The Debtor is required to pay all post-petition domestic support obligations directly to the holder of the claim and not through the Chapter 13 Plan.

1. Name of Debtor owing a domestic support obligation: _____

DSO Claimant Name	Address, City, State and ZIP	Estimated Arrearages	Current

B) Domestic Support Obligations Assigned to or Owed to a Governmental Unit Under 11 U.S.C. § 507(a)(1)(B):

Government Entity	Estimated Arrearages	Estimated Amount Paid	State Agency Case Number

C) Secured Income Tax Claims and Priority Claims Under 11 U.S.C. § 507:

All allowed secured tax obligations shall be paid in full by the Trustee as set forth herein. All allowed priority claims shall be paid in full by the Trustee as set forth herein, unless the creditor agrees otherwise:

Creditor	Priority/Secured	Estimated Claim Amount	Interest Rate (If Any)

8. *LONG–TERM DEBTS PAID DIRECTLY BY THE DEBTOR OR CO–DEBTOR TO THE CREDITOR*

Creditor	Basis for Treatment Claim	Estimated Claim Amount	Monthly Payment	Number of Payments Remaining

9. *AVOIDANCE OF LIENS*

The Debtor will file a separate motion or adversary proceeding to avoid the following non-purchase money security interests, judicial liens, wholly unsecured mortgages or other liens that impair exemptions, and the Trustee shall make no distributions thereon.

Creditor	Collateral/Property	Amount of Lien to be Avoided

10. *UNSECURED CLAIMS*

The minimum amount the Debtor must pay to all classes of allowed non-priority unsecured claims is _____ or ☐ 100%.

11. *POST PETITION CLAIMS*

Post-petition claims shall not be paid by the Trustee unless the Debtor amends the Plan to specifically address such claims. Absent such an amendment, the Trustee shall not disburse any monies on said claims and these debts will not be discharged.

12. *LIEN RETENTION*

With respect to each allowed secured claim to be paid in full through the Plan, other than mortgage or long-term debts, the holder of such claim shall retain the lien securing its claim until the earlier of (i) the payment of the underlying debt determined under non-bankruptcy law; or (ii) entry of the discharge order under 11 U.S.C. § 1328.

13. *PROOF OF LIEN PERFECTION*

Any individual and/or entity filing a secured claim must provide the Chapter 13 Trustee, the Debtor, and Debtor's counsel with proof of lien perfection at the time its claim is filed and shall attach such documentation to its Proof of Claim pursuant to Bankruptcy Rule 3001.

14. *VESTING OF PROPERTY OF THE ESTATE*

Property of the estate shall revest in the Debtor upon confirmation of the Debtor's Plan, subject to the rights, if any, of the Trustee to assert a claim to additional property of the estate acquired by Debtor post-petition pursuant to 11 U.S.C. § 1306.

15. *PAYMENT NOTICES*

Creditors in Section 3 of this Plan (whose rights are not being modified) and in Section 6 of this Plan (Assumed Executory Contracts/Unexpired Leases) may continue to mail customary notices or coupons to the Debtor or Trustee notwithstanding the automatic stay.

16. *OBJECTIONS TO CLAIMS*

Absent leave of Court, any objection to a timely filed general unsecured claim shall be filed within 45 days following the expiration of the claims bar date for that claim. Objections to secured and/or amended claims shall be filed within 45 days from the applicable claims bar date or within forty-five 45 days from the date of filing of the claim, whichever is later.

17. *STAY RELIEF*

Notwithstanding any provision contained herein to the contrary, distribution to a secured creditor(s) who obtains relief from the automatic stay will terminate immediately upon entry of an Order lifting or terminating the stay, except to the extent that an unsecured deficiency claim is subsequently filed and allowed. Absent an Order of the Court, relief from the automatic stay shall also result in the Trustee ceasing distribution to all junior lien holders.

18. *DEBTOR REFUNDS*

Upon written request of the Debtor, the Trustee is authorized to refund to the Debtor, without Court approval, any *erroneous* overpayment of *regular* monthly payments received during the term of the Plan that have not been previously disbursed.

19. *PLAN NOT ALTERED FROM OFFICIAL FORM*

By filing this Plan, the Debtor and the Debtor's counsel represent that the Plan is the official form authorized by the Court. Changes, additions or deletions to this Plan are permitted *only* with Leave of Court.

20. *REASON(S) FOR AMENDMENT(S)*

Set forth a brief, concise statement of the reason(s) for the amendment(s). In addition, if there is a substantial change to the proposed Plan payments, or if the Trustee so requests, file an amended Schedule I & J.

_____

_____

_____

_____

Signatures

x _____   Date: _____
Signature of Attorney for Debtor(s)

x _____   Date: _____

x _____   Date: _____
Signature(s) of Debtor(s) (required if not represented by an attorney, otherwise optional)

[Amended effective August 1, 2011; July 21, 2015.]

CHAPTER 13 PROCEDURES MANUAL

Accompanying the Uniform Chapter 13 Plan
Effective August 1, 2011
Revised July 21, 2015

This manual is divided into three parts. The first part governs general Chapter 13 practice within the Southern District of Illinois. The second part deals with the use and implementation of the new Uniform Chapter 13 Plan effective for all cases filed on or after August 1, 2011. The third part concerns new general requirements for Chapter 13 practice beginning with the implementation of the new Uniform Chapter 13 plan. All § references are to the Bankruptcy Code.

PART ONE—General Provisions Regarding Chapter 13 Practice

1) **Conflict of Laws.** If a conflict arises between the terms set forth in the Chapter 13 Procedures Manual and any bankruptcy rule, the national and local bankruptcy rule supersede the Chapter 13 Procedures Manual.

2) **Uniform Chapter 13 Plans.**

A) *Mandatory Model Plan.* For all Chapter 13 cases filed in the Southern District of Illinois, the Court requires the use of the most current Uniform Chapter 13 Plan in use on the date of filing the original petition. Anyone filing an Amended Plan must always use the same version of the Uniform Chapter 13 Plan in use when the case was filed. Changes, additions, or deletions to the Plan, other than to add or delete creditor line boxes, are strictly prohibited without leave of Court. Uniform Plans, as well as their effective dates, can be found on the Court's website at *www.ilsb.uscourts.gov/forms*.

A prior version of the Uniform (standard) Chapter 13 Plan used in this District contains the following sentence in section 4(C): "Any claim by the creditors listed below will be deemed satisfied in full through surrender of the collateral." Said sentence is null and void and shall have no further force or effect in Chapter 13 cases pending in this Court.

B) *Designation on Chapter 13 Plans.* Each Amended Plan shall be titled "Amended Plan No. 1," "Amended Plan No. 2," etc., as is appropriate.

3) **Signatures.** If debtor is represented by counsel, the debtor's signature is not required on chapter 13 plans filed with the Court. Counsel shall maintain some type of verification from debtor indicating the debtor's knowledge and approval of the plan as filed. Failure to do so will result in the imposition of sanctions by the Court, including but not limited to disgorgement of attorney fees.

4) **Minimum Monthly Chapter 13 Plan Payment.** Unless otherwise ordered, the minimum monthly Chapter 13 Plan payment is $100.00.

5) **Attorney's Fees for Cases that Convert to Chapter 7.** Upon conversion of a chapter 13 case to chapter 7, the chapter 13 trustee shall file with the Court a "Statement of Attorney's Fees Disbursed by the Chapter 13 Trustee."

6) **Compliance With the Filing Requirement of 11 U.S.C. § 521(A)(1).**

A) Copies of all payment advices, or other evidence of payment, received by the Debtor from any employer of the Debtor within 60 days prior to the date of the filing of the bankruptcy petition (i) shall not be filed with the Court unless otherwise ordered and (ii) shall be provided to the Trustee, the United States Trustee if no Trustee has been appointed, and to any creditor who timely requests copies of them, at least seven days before the § 341 meeting of creditors. To be considered timely, a creditor's request must be received at least 14 days before the first date set for the meeting of creditors.

B) The requirements of § 521(a)(1)(B)(iv) (copies of all payment advices or other evidence of payment received within 60 days before the date of the filing of the petition by the Debtor from any employer of the Debtor) are satisfied by providing to the Trustee, or the United States Trustee in a case where no Trustee has been appointed, at least seven days before the first date set for the § 341 meeting:

1) Payment advices or other evidence of payment. This requirement may be satisfied by providing less than "all payment advices or other evidence of payment received within 60 days before the date of the filing of the petition ..." by, for example, providing a year-to-date statement that includes payments received within 60 days of the petition; or

2) A verified statement that the Debtor did not receive payments to which § 521(a)(1)(B)(iv) applies.

Pay advices or other evidence of payment shall be arranged (a) separately for each debtor and (b) chronologically for each different employer. Notwithstanding the foregoing, the Trustee may require that six months of pay advices or other evidence of payment as defined in subparagraph (1) above be provided to verify the current monthly income listed on Official Form B22A or B22C. Failure to provide this documentation shall not delay the commencement of the § 341 meeting of creditors.

In no event shall the documents required by § 521(a)(1)(B)(iv) be provided later than 45 days after the date of the filing of the petition. If the § 341 meeting is not set within 45 days of the filing of the petition, the 45–day deadline for providing payment advices to the Trustee (or the United States Trustee if applicable) still applies. If the Trustee or the United States Trustee continues the § 341 meeting to receive these documents, such continuance shall *not* be deemed a request or consent to extend the deadline of § 521(i). Nothing in this section is to be construed as requiring the Trustee or the United States Trustee to continue the § 341 meeting.

Failure to provide the documents within the 45–day deadline is grounds for the Trustee (or the United States Trustee if applicable) to request dismissal. If the case is dismissed following such a request by the Trustee or the United States Trustee, and the Debtor believes the case was dismissed in error, the Debtor shall file any motion to reinstate the case within 14 days of the entry of the dismissal order. A case that has been dismissed for failure to file a required document or provide a required document to the Trustee or the United States Trustee will not be considered to be a case dismissed in error.

C) *11 U.S.C. § 521(a)(1)(B)(v).* The requirement of § 521(a)(1)(B)(v) (statement of the amount of monthly net income itemized to show how the amount is calculated) is satisfied by including such information on the Debtor's Schedule I.

D) *11 U.S.C. § 521(a)(1)(B)(vi).* The requirement of § 521(a)(1)(B)(vi) (a statement disclosing any reasonably anticipated increase in income or expenditures over the 12–month period following the date of the filing of the petition) is satisfied by including such information on the appropriate line of Schedule J.

7) Continuance of the § 341 Meeting Announced at the Meeting. The Trustee or the United States Trustee may continue a § 341 meeting by announcement at the meeting. The Trustee or the United States Trustee shall list the continued date, time, and location for the continued meeting by making a docket entry using the Court's CM/ECF system. No further notice of the continued date is required. Unless otherwise agreed, the continued § 341 meeting will be set no earlier than 7 days after the prior § 341 meeting.

8) Chapter 13 Plans: Confirmation Procedures.

A) *Deadline to File Objections to Confirmation of Plan and Original Confirmation Hearing.* A confirmation hearing will be scheduled by the Court at the time of scheduling the § 341 meeting of creditors. Notice of the confirmation hearing will be included on the § 341 Meeting of Creditors Notice. In the event the § 341 meeting is continued, the Court will continue the confirmation hearing and provide notice thereof. An objection to the original Plan is considered timely if filed and served within 21 days after the date the § 341 meeting of creditors is concluded. Timely filed objections to confirmation, whether by a creditor or the Chapter 13 Trustee, will be heard at the confirmation hearing unless an order resolving the objection is entered prior to the scheduled confirmation hearing or an Amended Plan has been filed.

Objections to Amended Plans filed prior to confirmation must be filed and served within 21 days after the date of filing the Amended Plan and will be scheduled for hearing by the Court.

Untimely objections may be summarily denied by the Court.

B) *Attendance at Confirmation Hearings.* The Trustee or counsel for the Trustee shall attend all confirmation hearings unless (1) previously excused by the Court; (2) an Order has been entered on all objections to confirmation; or (3) an Amended Plan has been filed. The Debtor's attorney or the Debtor, if not represented by an attorney, and any party objecting to confirmation, shall attend the hearing if objections have been filed and are still pending. The parties may contact the courtroom deputy in order to request an excused absence if an agreement has been reached prior to the hearing date, and if the Court is informed of this agreement by 3:30 p.m. the business day before the hearing. Absent such an excuse, failure to appear at the confirmation hearing may result in the overruling of the objection, or the denial of confirmation, and may subject counsel to further sanctions by the Court.

C) *Settlement Conference.*

1) Creditor Objections. At least 10 days prior to the hearing on the objection to confirmation of the plan, the parties shall meet and discuss possible resolution of the objection. The burden of scheduling this meeting shall be on debtors' counsel.

2) Trustee Objections. In cases where the trustee files an objection to confirmation, the trustee shall schedule a settlement conference to discuss possible resolution of the objection. Notice of the settlement conference shall be posted on the trustee's website at least 10 days prior to the scheduled conference. All parties shall be prepared to conduct a meaningful settlement conference on the date and at the time scheduled by the trustee. If the debtor has no factual or legal basis on which to dispute the objection(s) raised by the trustee, the debtor shall file the necessary pleadings/documents to cure the objection(s) no later than the date and time of the scheduled settlement conference.

Within two days following the settlement conference, debtor's counsel shall advise the Court (by email) of those matters which have been resolved. Failure of the parties to comply with any of these provisions may result in the imposition of sanctions, including the reduction of attorney's fees.

D) *Amended Plans Filed Prior to Confirmation in Response to Objections.* If the Debtor has no legal or factual basis to dispute the objection filed by the Trustee or a creditor, the Debtor shall file those documents necessary to cure the objection as soon as possible so as to expedite the confirmation process.

E) *Actions That Will Moot Pending Objections to Confirmation.*

1) Amended Plans. The filing of an Amended Plan moots any pending objections to a previously filed Plan. If an Amended Plan is filed prior to the confirmation hearing scheduled on the original plan, the confirmation hearing date is canceled. If objections to a Plan are scheduled for hearing and an Amended Plan is filed, the hearing will be stricken from the docket upon either of the following: (1) entry of an Order mooting the objection, (2) counsel calling the Court and being excused from appearing. Nothing in this section is to be construed to prohibit an interested party from filing an objection to the Amended Plan.

2) Amended Objections to Plans. If a party files an amended objection to a Plan, any previous objections filed by that party are deemed moot. The Court will consider only those matters which have been raised in the amended objection.

3) Confirmation. If the Chapter 13 Trustee files a recommendation to confirm a Plan or orally recommends confirmation, that recommendation moots any objections previously filed by the Trustee.

F) *The Trustee's "Recommendation to Confirm" (East St. Louis) or "No Objection" (Benton) Filed Prior to Confirmation.* If the Trustee, after having reviewed the petition, schedules and Chapter 13 Plan, and after examining the Debtor at the § 341 meeting of creditors to ensure compliance with §§ 1322 and 1325, has no objection to a Plan prior to confirmation, whether an original or Amended Plan, he or she shall file a "Recommendation to Confirm" or "No Objection" to the relevant Plan. Such filing is to reference whether it is filed in response to an original Plan or an Amended Plan and, if an Amended Plan, the appropriate number listed on the Amended Plan. While it depends on the Trustee as to which named document is filed, this document shall be docketed as a Recommendation to Confirm. Such document shall be filed not later than 21 days after the conclusion of the § 341 meeting of creditors or, in the case of an Amended Plan filed prior to confirmation, within 21 days after the filing of the Amended Plan.

G) *Confirmation of Plan.* In the event no objections to the original plan are filed, the scheduled confirmation hearing will be held, at which time the Court may enter an order of confirmation. Upon the expiration of the time for objecting to an Amended Plan and/or the resolution of all pending objections to a Plan or an Amended Plan, the Court may enter an order of confirmation, whether or not the Trustee's Recommendation to Confirm has been filed.

9) Amended Plans.

A) *Generally.* Any amended or modified plan filed with the Court must be captioned as an "Amended Plan" and must indicate the "Amended Plan Number" (e.g., "Amended Plan No. 1"). The amended plan must contain all provisions of the plan. Motions seeking to amend only certain provisions of the plan will be summarily denied.

B) *Identification of Amendments.* Amendments to a Plan *must* be underlined if being added/modified or *lined through* if being deleted. Failure to identify any changes will result in the plan being noticed as deficient by the Clerk's office.

C) *Post–Confirmation Amended Plans Curing Delinquent Payments.* Any post-confirmation Amended Plans curing delinquent payments shall be filed in conformity with Sections 17(A) and 17(B) below governing Plan payment delinquency. Such plans shall include a "Total Paid In" (TPI) amount to be listed in the first tier of the funding provision by using the month number.

10) Service of Original and Amended Plans.

A) *Original Plans.*

1) Filed With the Petition. Notwithstanding any provision of the Local Rules, the Chapter 13 Trustee is responsible for serving a copy of the original Plan, as filed with the Clerk of the Court, on all creditors listed in the Debtor's schedules, provided that said Plan is filed contemporaneously with the petition.

2) Not Filed With the Petition. If the Plan is not filed with the petition, the Debtor shall serve a copy of the Plan on all parties listed on the Debtor's mailing matrix and file a certificate of service with the Court.

B) *Amended Plans Filed Prior to Confirmation.*

1) If the claims bar date found in Bankruptcy Rule 3002(c) has not yet expired, the Debtor shall serve a copy of each Amended Plan on the Trustee, all creditors, and all parties listed on the Debtor's mailing matrix.

2) If the claims bar date found in Bankruptcy Rule 3002(c) has expired, the Debtor shall serve a copy of each Amended Plan on the Trustee, all parties who have filed a claim or a request for service, all secured creditors, or as otherwise required by this Manual.

C) *Post–Confirmation Modifications.*

1) If the claims bar date found in Bankruptcy Rule 3002(c) has not yet expired, the Debtor shall serve a copy of each Amended Plan on the Trustee, all creditors, and all parties listed on the Debtor's mailing matrix.

2) If the claims bar date found in Bankruptcy Rule 3002(c) has expired, the Debtor shall serve a copy of each Amended Plan on the Trustee, all parties who have filed a claim or a request for service, all secured creditors, or as otherwise required by this Manual.

3) Debtor shall also file amended Schedules I and J to demonstrate that the Amended Plan is filed in good faith.

(D) *Limited Service of Certain Amended Plans.* Except as indicated in (iii) below, service of an Amended Plan may be limited to the Trustee if the proposed Amended Plan meets one of the following criteria:

1) The proposed Plan only changes the terms of the Plan by increasing the amount of the Plan payment or Plan duration; or,

2) The proposed Plan:

(i) Corrects errors in the funding paragraph; or

(ii) Changes the employer information;

(iii) Corrects collateral information due to typographical error (in this instance, the affected creditor must also be noticed);

(iv) Corrects any other scrivener's or mathematical errors that will not adversely and materially affect the timing, amount, and total payment on allowed claims; or

(v) Does not waive any missed plan payments.

If limited service is authorized, the front page of the Plan must so indicate by checking the box "Limited Service Applicable." If limited service is used and the box is not marked, the Clerk of Court will process the Plan as deficient.

11) Objections to Plans Amended After Confirmation.

A) *Creditors.* Objections to Plans amended after confirmation shall be filed with the Court and served upon the Debtor, the Debtor's attorney (if any), and the Trustee no later than 21 days after the date the Amended Plan is filed.

B) *Chapter 13 Trustee.* The Trustee shall file, no later than 21 days after the date the Amended Plan is filed, a pleading either recommending approval of the Plan or objecting to it, referencing the specific modification number listed on the Plan.

C) *Moot Objections.* See Section 8(E).

D) *Attendance at Hearings on Objections to Plans Amended After Confirmation.* The Debtor's attorney or the Debtor, if not represented by an attorney, and any party objecting to the Amended Plan shall attend the hearing set on such objections. The parties may contact the courtroom deputy in order to request an excused absence if an agreement has been reached prior to the hearing date, and if the Court is informed of this agreement by 3:30 p.m. the business day before the hearing. Absent such an excuse, failure to appear at the hearing may result in the entry of an order overruling the objection or entry of an order denying approval of the Amended Plan, and may subject counsel to further sanctions by the Court.

12) How Chapter 13 Trustee Disbursements are Affected by the Timing of the Filing of an Amended Plan. If a modification of a Plan is received in the Trustee's office not later than three business days prior to the Trustee's next disbursement cycle, the Trustee is authorized, but not required, to distribute funds in accordance with the terms of the proposed modification commencing with that next disbursement, notwithstanding that an Order approving the modification has not yet been entered. Upon request of the Trustee, the Clerk of Court shall issue any wage deduction order consistent with such modification.

In the event that a Plan provision calls for the surrender of collateral on which the Trustee has been making payments, the Trustee shall reserve funds to that creditor until such time as the Order approving the modification is entered, at which time the reserve shall be released and funds distributed to other creditors pursuant to the modification of the Plan.

13) Distribution by the Chapter 13 Trustee in Circumstances of Insufficient Funds. In those circumstances where there are insufficient funds on hand to disburse the monthly payment amount, the Chapter 13 Trustee is authorized to disburse those funds pursuant to the Order of Distribution in the Uniform Plan in effect at that time.

14) Calculation of the Chapter 13 Trustee Fee. In calculating the amount of the Trustee's fee, the Debtor shall use the Chapter 13 Trustee's "effective percentage fee" in effect at the time the Plan is filed. It is the responsibility of counsel for the Debtor to monitor any changes in the fee and, if necessary, to amend the Plan to reflect any increase or decrease in the fee. The "effective percentage fee" is the fee based on the percentage allowed by the United States Trustee adjusted for certain factors (e.g. the Trustee's fee to pay the Trustee's fee). This information is available from each individual Trustee.

15) Chapter 13 Claim Objections. Absent leave of Court, any objection to a timely filed unsecured claim shall be filed within 45 days following the expiration of the claims bar date for that claim. Objections to secured and/or amended claims shall be filed within 45 days from the applicable claims bar date or within 45 days from the date of filing of the claim, whichever is later.

An objection to a proof of claim in a Chapter 13 case shall be served upon the claimant, any attorney who filed an entry of appearance for the claimant, the Trustee, the Debtor, and the Debtor's attorney (if any). Objections to claims in Chapter 13 cases will be heard only if a timely response in opposition is filed with the Court. The notice of objection shall state that any responsive pleading shall be filed with the Court, with a copy forwarded to all interested parties, no later than 30 days of the date of the notice, and that if no response is filed, the Court will enter an order sustaining the objection and disallowing or modifying the claim without further notice to any party.

16) Discharge in Chapter 13 Cases (Applicable only to cases filed on or after October 17, 2005).

A) *Trustee's Notice of Completion.* The Chapter 13 Trustee shall file a "Report of Plan Completion, Request for Termination of Wage Order and Notice Concerning Discharge" ("Trustee's Report/Notice") after all payments have been received.

B) *The Debtor's Required Pleadings.* *Within 21 days of the filing of the Trustee's Report/Notice, eligible Debtors shall file a Motion and Notice to all creditors and parties in interest, pursuant to 11 U.S.C. § 1328 and Bankruptcy Rule 2002(f), setting forth their eligibility for discharge. Failure to timely file said Motion and Notice will result in the Clerk of the Court closing this case without entry of an Order of Discharge.

*Prior to filing said Motion and Notice, the Debtor's counsel shall verify Debtor's eligibility to receive a discharge pursuant to 11 U.S.C. § 1328.

C) *Closing and Reopening.* If the case is closed due to an eligible Debtor's failure to timely file the Motion and Notice as required by subparagraph B above, and the Motion and Notice are subsequently filed after the case has been closed, the Debtor must also simultaneously file a Motion to Reopen Case with the required filing fee. The Motion to Reopen must set forth the reason(s) the case was closed without discharge.

(17) Delinquent Plan Payments. *Trustee's Notice of Default in Plan Payments and Options to Cure.*

A) Upon a determination by the Chapter 13 Trustee that plan payments are delinquent, prior to the filing of a Motion to Dismiss for Failure to Make Plan Payments, the Trustee shall provide the Debtor and the Debtor's counsel (if any) with written notice of any default and options to cure. Within 45 days thereafter, debtor(s) must exercise one of the following three options:

1) Make payment to the Trustee;

2) Enter into an Agreed Order, to be submitted to the Court, setting forth the manner in which the arrearages shall be cured and requiring future Plan payments to remain current for an agreed upon period of time; or

3) File an Amended Plan with the Court, curing the delinquency. Note that, absent extraordinary circumstances, this option is not available if another Plan curing the delinquency has been filed within the past 12 months.

B) Failure by the Debtor to implement one of the foregoing options within 45 days will result in the Trustee filing a Motion to Dismiss with the Court. Upon review of the Trustee's motion, the Court may dismiss the case without further notice or hearing.

18) **Motions to Reinstate Following Dismissal on the Trustee's Motion to Dismiss for Failure to Make Plan Payments.** The motion shall state whether the case was previously dismissed and reinstated and shall provide dates of any prior dismissals and orders of reinstatement and the proposed manner in which the arrearage is to be cured. The Debtor shall serve a copy of the motion on the Trustee, U.S. Trustee, and all parties in interest.

19) **Monthly Operating Reports in Chapter 13.** Unless required by the Chapter 13 Trustee, § 1304(c) shall not apply.

20) **Obtaining Credit in Chapter 13 Cases.**

A) *Dollar Limits.* The Debtor may incur non-emergency, consumer debt up to $1,000.00 without written approval of the Trustee or Order of the Court. Non–emergency, consumer debt exceeding $1,000.00 requires the approval of the Trustee or an Order of the Court, using the procedures set forth in subparagraphs (B) and (C) below. Notwithstanding the foregoing, nothing shall prevent the Debtor from incurring reasonable and necessary medical expenses.

B) *Request Directed to Trustee.* The Debtor shall first request approval to incur debt by written application to the Trustee. Such request shall not be filed with the Court. If approved by the Trustee, the Debtor may incur the debt in accordance with the terms and conditions approved by the Trustee. If the Trustee has not directed use of a specific form, the application shall include the following information:

1) A statement of facts (or a proposed amended Schedule I and J) in support of the feasibility of the request;

2) A description of the item to be purchased or the collateral affected by the credit to be obtained;

3) The reasons why the Debtor has need for the credit; and

4) The terms of any financing involved, including the interest rate.

C) *Motion Directed to Court.* If the request is not approved by the Trustee, the Debtor may file a Motion to Incur Debt. The motion shall contain all of the information required to be included in the request by subparagraph (B) above and shall state that the Trustee has denied the request. The motion should be served on the Trustee.

21) **Compliance with Requests for Information from the Chapter 13 Trustee.** To assist the Trustee in determining compliance with the "best interest of creditors" test for confirmation of Chapter 13 Plans (*see 11 U.S.C. § 1325(a)(4)*), the Trustee may require that the Debtor submit a liquidation analysis, showing that the proposed distribution to unsecured creditors under the Plan is not less than the amount such creditors would receive in a Chapter 7 liquidation. Such information shall be provided to the Trustee within 10 days of his request. The failure to comply with the Trustee's request may be grounds for dismissal of the Debtor's case.

PART TWO—Specific Provisions of the Uniform Chapter 13 Plan for All Cases Filed On or After August 1, 2011

Claims Based Plan With Exceptions. Generally, this is a "claims based" Plan. As such, all allowed secured and priority claims will be paid the amount of their allowed secured/priority claim, except as provided in paragraph 4(B) of the Plan. The interest rate set forth in the Plan shall be binding on all parties upon confirmation/approval of the same Plan unless a timely written objection is filed.

1) **Payments.** This section establishes the payment schedule the Debtor will use to make his or her Plan payments. The first "Start Month #" will always be "1" and the "End Month #" will be the last month in which the Debtor will make that specific dollar amount of a monthly payment. The "Plan Payment Amount" is the monthly payment.

For example, if the Debtor proposes a 48–month plan, the "Start Month #" will be "1", the "End Month #" will be "48", and the total will be the Plan Payment Amount multiplied by 48. The additional lines will be utilized in circumstances where there is an unusual payment (e.g. lawsuit proceeds), the Plan Payment Amount changes due to a subsequent amendment, or in those certain circumstances where a step payment may be justified. An example is shown below:

Start Month	#End Month	#Monthly Payment	Total
1	33	200.00	6,600.00
34	60	300.00	8,100.00
Unknown lawsuit proceeds		Estimated	15,000.00
Total Months: 60		Grand Total Payments: 29,700.00	

The Debtor's employment information is self-explanatory. Absent leave of Court, entry of a wage withholding order is mandatory in all cases unless the Debtor's sole source of income is (i) Social Security benefits, (ii) retirement funds, (iii) unemployment benefits, (iv) self-employment, or (v) family assistance.

If the Debtor is amending the Plan to cure an arrearage in payments, the Debtor must so indicate in this section.

Order of Distribution. This sets forth the priority of payments to creditors. Unless the higher distribution level is an ongoing contractual monthly payment, all creditors must be paid in full in each category before disbursements will be made in a lower distribution level.

The first parties to be paid are the Court for any unpaid filing fees and the Chapter 13 Trustee's fees, including those for notice and mailing. Following the payment of these fees, ongoing monthly mortgage payments due after the Plan is filed will be paid. Treatment and payment of the monthly mortgage payments is set forth in greater detail below. Following mortgage payments, allowed administrative expenses will be paid. Following administrative expenses, attorney's fees and other secured creditors will be paid. The amount disbursed to each will be calculated as follows:

Based upon allowed secured claims, the attorney will receive ½ of the monies disbursed and the remaining ½ of the monies disbursed will be paid to allowed secured creditors on a pro rata basis. Pre-confirmation, the attorney shall not be entitled to receive more than $2,500.00 of their attorney's fees. Thereafter, commencing with the next regular disbursement and using the same disbursement calculation described above, the Trustee shall begin reserving the monies to be paid to the attorney until such time as the case has been confirmed. With the first regular disbursement after the case is confirmed, the Trustee shall release all funds on hold to the attorney and continue making monthly disbursements to the attorney until the remainder of the attorney's fees has been paid in full. Once the Debtor's attorney's fees have been paid in full, the secured creditors will begin to receive all the funds available, on a pro rata basis, until such time as each secured creditor's claim is paid in full. In those cases in which there are no secured creditors, the Debtor's attorney will be paid the entire amount of the monies to be disbursed each month until their fees are paid in full, subject to the pre-confirmation limit set forth above.

Following payment of attorney's fees and secured claims, the Trustee shall pay priority claims, followed by special classes of unsecured creditors as stated in the Plan and, finally, general unsecured creditors.

Interim Disbursements by the Chapter 13 Trustee as Adequate Protection Payments under 11 U.S.C. § 1326(a)(1)(C). Commencing with the first regular disbursement after the conclusion of the Debtor's § 341 meeting of creditors, the Chapter 13 Trustee shall begin disbursement of the regular Plan payments received from, or on behalf of, the Debtor, to allowed claims pursuant to the Order of Distribution set forth in the Uniform Chapter 13 Plan.

2) **Administrative Expenses.**

Administrative Creditor. For any allowed claim to be paid as an administrative expense, the Creditor's name and the estimated amount of the claim must be included in this section.

Attorney's Fees and Responsibilities. The Debtor shall indicate in this section whether the Debtor's attorney shall be paid a flat rate for representation during the entire case (with certain exceptions) or by filing a fee application. Once a Debtor elects either section, the Debtor is bound by the selection throughout the bankruptcy case, unless on motion, the Court orders otherwise.

A) *Flat Fees.* Effective for cases filed on or after January 19, 2011, if the Debtor elects to pay the attorney's fees on a flat fee schedule, then the maximum allowable flat fee for a non-business related bankruptcy is $4,000.00. The maximum flat fee for a business related bankruptcy is $4,500.00. A business bankruptcy is one in which the Debtor is engaged in business as defined by § 1304(a). Effective for cases filed October 17, 2005 through January 18, 2011, the maximum allowable flat fee is $3,500.00 for a non-business related bankruptcy and $4,000.00 for a business bankruptcy.

Upon notice, and if necessary, a hearing, the Court may award additional attorney's fees for the defense or prosecution of adversary proceedings by approving a fee application filed pursuant to the standards set forth by this Court in *In re Wiedau's, Inc.*, 78 B.R. 904 (Bankr.S.D.Ill.1987). Upon entry of such an award, the Plan shall be amended to pay such additional fees pursuant to the same terms set forth in the Order of Distribution.

B) *Hourly Fees.* Attorneys electing to be paid on an hourly basis must file a fee application for approval of fees. No fees shall be disbursed until a fee application is approved by the Court. However, the Trustee shall reserve a total of $4,000.00 for payment toward such application pursuant to the terms concerning payment of the attorney's fees as set forth in the Order of Distribution. The fee application must be made pursuant to the standards set forth by this Court in *In re Wiedau's, Inc.*, 78 B.R. 904 (Bankr.S.D.Ill.1987).

C) *The Debtor's and Attorney's Rights and Responsibilities.* Each Debtor and his or her counsel must execute a Rights and Responsibilities Form setting forth the minimum preparation and duties to be performed by the Debtor's counsel throughout the Chapter 13 bankruptcy. *See Appendix A.*

Failure to meet the requirements of the Rights and Responsibilities Form may result in any sanction the Court finds appropriate and reasonable under the circumstances including, but not limited to, disgorgement of fees and/or suspension of the attorney's right to practice before the Bankruptcy Court in this District.

Executed copies of this form shall be supplied upon request to the Court, the Chapter 13 Trustee, or the United States Trustee.

A Rule 2016(b) (Disclosure of Compensation of Attorney for Debtor) must be filed by every attorney entering an appearance on behalf of the Debtor. Care should be taken to ensure that the disclosures on this form are consistent with the attorney's fee amounts requested in the Chapter 13 Uniform Plan. This disclosure is a continuing obligation and must be updated during the pendency of the case to list any subsequent fees received by counsel directly from, or on behalf of, the Debtor, excluding those payments received from the Trustee pursuant to the terms of the Debtor's Plan.

3) Real Estate—Curing Defaults and Maintaining Payments.

A) *Payment of Ongoing Mortgage Payments by the Trustee and Calculation of Pre-petition Mortgage Arrearage.* Post-petition payments shall be made by the Trustee if (i) a pre-petition default exists, (ii) a post-petition, pre-confirmation default occurs, or (iii) a post-confirmation default arises that cannot be cured by the Debtor within six months. Otherwise, post-petition payments may be made directly by the Debtor to the creditor. Where the Trustee is disbursing the ongoing payments, the first mortgage payment to be disbursed will be that which becomes due in the second month after the month in which the petition is filed. In this situation, a mortgage holder should file a "pre-petition" claim that includes both the pre-petition arrearage and all post-petition contractual payments not disbursed by the Trustee as set forth above. Similarly, the Debtor must include the amount of any such payment in the pre-petition arrearage calculation.

When the Trustee is to act as disbursing agent for the ongoing mortgage payments at the commencement of the case, the Debtor shall calculate any arrearage to include all post-petition payments that have become due from the date of filing up to and including the last day of the following month. For example, if a case is commenced on January 3rd (or any other month), the post-petition arrearage shall include all payments that come due from January 4th up to and including any payments that are to become due through the last day of February. Thus, assuming the Debtor's mortgage payment was due on the 10th of the month, the number of post-petition payments to be included in the arrearage would be two—the payment due on January 10th and the payment due on February 10th. Thereafter, the Trustee would start disbursing the ongoing mortgage payments commencing with the March 10th payment. *See Table Below.*

Filing Date	Mortgage Due Date	# Post–Petition Payments Included in Arrears Claim	# Mortgage Payments Disbursed by Trustee
3rd day of Month	1st day of Month	1	Proposed plan duration
3rd day of Month	10th day of Month	2	Proposed plan duration

As the Trustee disburses payment of ongoing mortgage payments with the prior month's disbursement (i.e. the April mortgage payment is paid with the March disbursement [further assuming funds are available, the § 341 meeting has been concluded, and the creditor has an allowed claim on file]), the number of ongoing mortgage payments to be disbursed by the Trustee would equal the proposed length of the Plan—i.e. for a 36 month Plan, the Trustee would disburse 36 ongoing mortgage payments.

If the Plan is subsequently amended to have the Trustee act as disbursing agent (i.e. the Debtor was initially making the payments directly), the payments by the Trustee are to begin on the first due date after the month in which the amended or modified Plan is filed or as otherwise ordered by the Court.

It shall be the duty of the Debtor(s) and his or her counsel to closely review each proof of claim filed by or on behalf of a mortgage company to ensure that said entity properly and correctly included any of the aforementioned payments in their arrearage claim.

No late charges, fees or other monetary amounts shall be assessed based on the timing of any payments made by the Trustee under the provisions of the Plan unless allowed by Order of the Court.

B) *The Amount of the Monthly Mortgage Payment.* If the Trustee is required to make current monthly payments, the Trustee is to pay the current monthly payment, as increased or decreased, as stated by the mortgage company in their original proof of claim and pursuant to any subsequent claim supplements. In the event the proof of claim does not set forth a current monthly payment amount, the Trustee shall pay the amount as set forth in the Debtor's plan.

C) *Monthly Mortgage Payment Change.* General Order 08–3 is repealed effective December 1, 2011.

D) *Payment of Pre–Petition Arrearages.* Absent an objection, the Trustee shall use the amount of the pre-petition arrearage listed in the mortgage holder's proof of claim.

E) *Payment of Post–Petition Arrearages.* The Debtor may propose an Amended Plan that seeks to pay, as a separate claim, any post-petition mortgage payments that have accrued after the date of the filing of the petition.

1) Subparagraph 3(C) of the Plan should be used for post-petition arrearages *only* when the Debtor seeks to include post-petition mortgage arrearages arising as a result of the Debtor's failure to timely pay such payments directly outside their Chapter 13 Plan.

2) Subparagraph 3(D) of the Plan should be used for post-petition mortgage arrears *only* (i) when the ongoing mortgage payments at issue were being disbursed by the Chapter 13 Trustee and (ii) the post-petition arrearage arises from a default by the Debtor in the Plan payments.

Unless otherwise indicated, the use of subparagraph 3(D) of the Plan constitutes an affirmative representation by the filing party that the Debtor and the affected creditor have agreed to have this post-petition arrearage paid as a separate claim. Prior to filing this Plan, the Debtor must use diligent efforts to attempt to contact the creditor to more accurately determine the arrearage, to avoid challenges to this treatment of post-petition mortgage arrearages and to make the process of approval of the Plan more efficient. At a minimum, the Debtor should attempt to contact the affected creditor and/or their counsel, if known, at least two times in writing and two times by phone using the best possible contact information before proceeding with the filing of an Amended Plan that proposes such treatment of their claim.

If, after making diligent efforts, the Debtor is unable to contact the creditor, the Debtor may represent that he or she has made reasonable and diligent efforts to secure an agreement with the creditor for the above-described treatment of this post-petition arrearage. This is done by checking the box in the plan. Further, upon request by any party in interest, the filing party shall provide a detailed written explanation of the steps taken to attempt to secure an agreement with the creditor. Abuse of the letter and spirit of this provision may subject the filing party to any sanctions the Court deems appropriate.

3) If attorney's fees are being sought in conjunction with this post-petition arrearage, a separate Agreed Order and supplemental proof of claim for the fees must be filed with the Court.

F) *Notice Relating to Claims Secured by a Security Interest in the Debtor's Principal Residence and Non-residential Mortgages.*

1) In General. This section applies in a Chapter 13 case to claims that are (i) secured by a security interest in the Debtor's principal residence and (ii) provided for under § 1322(b)(5) in the Plan.

2) Notice of Payment Changes. **Rule 3002.1 of the Federal Rules of Bankruptcy Procedure also applies to nonresidential mortgages.**

The holder of the claim shall file and serve on the Debtor, the Debtor's counsel, and the Trustee a notice of any change in the payment amount, including any change that results from an interest rate or escrow account adjustment, no later than 21 days before a payment in the new amount is due.

(i) Upon filing of a Mortgagee's Notice, the Chapter 13 Trustee is authorized to commence disbursement of the payment amount set forth in the Mortgagee's Notice without the necessity of an Amended Plan having been filed, unless an objection to the Mortgagee's Notice is filed within twenty-one (21) days from the date the Mortgagee's Notice is filed. Should the Debtor(s) object to the Mortgagee's Notice, the Trustee shall reserve payment on the increased portion of the payment amount set forth in the Mortgagee's Notice until the objection is disposed of by the Court. This paragraph applies notwithstanding any Plan provision to the contrary, and regardless of the Plan version utilized by the Debtor(s).

(ii) If the Trustee subsequently determines any filed increase in the amount of the ongoing mortgage payment results in there being insufficient funding in the Plan to pay all classes of claims as required, the Trustee shall file a notice with the Court, or alternatively contact Debtor's counsel, alerting the parties of the failure of the Chapter 13 Plan to complete. If the Debtor fails to take any action with regard to the notice, the Trustee may seek dismissal of the case at the conclusion of the Plan term. Notwithstanding the foregoing, if any single payment change filed by the mortgage company results in an increase of the ongoing payment by more than $25.00 and no objection is filed by the Debtor within twenty-one (21) days from the date of the Mortgagee's Notice, a plan modification is required, whether filed by the Trustee or the Debtor. Said modification shall increase the Debtor's Plan payment and base amount accordingly. The Mortgage Payment Modification form can be obtained on the Court's website at www.ilsb.uscourts.gov.

3) Notice of Fees, Expenses and Charges. The holder of the claim shall file and serve on the Debtor, the Debtor's counsel, and the Trustee a notice itemizing all fees, expenses or charges (i) that were incurred in connection with the claim after the bankruptcy case was filed and (ii) that the holder asserts are recoverable against the Debtor or against the Debtor's principal residence. The notice shall be served as soon as practical, and in no event, not later than the earlier of 180 days after the date on which the fees, expenses, or charges are incurred, or the date the case is closed.

4) Form and Content. A notice filed and served under subdivision (2) or (3) of this section shall be prepared as prescribed by the appropriate Official Form and filed as a supplement to the holder's proof of claim. The notice is not subject to Rule 3001(f).

5) Determination of Fees, Expenses or Charges. On motion of the Debtor or the Trustee filed within one year after service of a notice under subdivision (3) of this section, the Court shall, after notice and hearing, determine whether payment of any claimed fee, expense, or charge is required by the underlying agreement and applicable non-bankruptcy law to cure a default or maintain payments in accordance with § 1322(b)(5) of the Bankruptcy Code.

6) Notice of Final Cure Payment. Within 30 days after the Debtor completes all payments under the Plan, the Trustee shall file and serve on the holder of the claim, the Debtor, and the Debtor's counsel a notice stating that the Debtor has paid in full the amount required to cure any default on the claim. The notice shall also inform the holder of its obligation to file and serve a response under subdivision (7) of this section. If the Debtor contends that a final cure payment has been made and all Plan payments have been completed and the Trustee does not timely file and serve the notice required by this subdivision, the Debtor may file and serve the notice.

7) Response to Notice of Final Cure Payment. Within 21 days after service of the notice under subdivision (6) of this section, the holder shall file and serve on the Debtor, the Debtor's counsel, and the Trustee a statement indicating (i) whether it agrees that the Debtor has paid in full the amount required to cure the default on the claim and (ii) whether the Debtor is otherwise current on all payments consistent with § 1322(b)(5). The statement shall itemize the required cure or post-petition amounts, if any, that the holder contends remain unpaid as of the date of the statement. The statement shall be filed as a supplement to the holder's proof of claim and is not subject to Rule 3001(f).

8) Determination of Final Cure and Payment. On motion of the Debtor or Trustee, filed within 21 days after service of the statement under subdivision (7) above, the Court shall, after notice and hearing, determine whether the Debtor has cured the default and paid all required post-petition amounts.

9) Failure to Notify. If the holder of a claim fails to provide any information as required by subdivision (2), (3), or (7) of this rule, the Court may, after notice and hearing, take either or both of the following actions:

(i) Preclude the holder from presenting the omitted information, in any form, as evidence in any contested matter or adversary proceeding in the case, unless the Court determines that the failure was substantially justified or harmless; or

(ii) Award other appropriate relief including reasonable expenses and attorney's fees caused by the failure.

G) *Motions for Relief from the Automatic Stay of 11 U.S.C. §§ 362 and 1301 when Leases or Mortgages are Being Paid Directly by the Debtor.* If the Debtor is making direct, ongoing, post-petition payments to the lessor or mortgagee and the lessor or mortgagee subsequently seeks relief from the automatic stay based upon an alleged default in such direct payments by the Debtor, the parties shall comply with the following requirements:

1) The parties shall exchange any and all documentary evidence concerning the post-petition payment history of the Debtor at least 7 days prior to the preliminary hearing on the Motion for Relief; and

2) The parties shall have such evidence available at the preliminary hearing for presentation to the Court.

3) The failure to comply with the requirements of sub-paragraphs (1) and (2) may result in the Court taking such action as it deems appropriate, which may include the granting or denying of the relief sought in the Motion for Relief.

H) *Motions for Relief from the Automatic Stays of 11 U.S.C. §§ 362 and 1301 when Mortgages are Being Paid by the Trustee.* If the Debtor's Plan proposes that the Trustee act as disbursing agent for ongoing mortgage payments and the mortgagee subsequently seeks relief from the automatic stay based upon an alleged default in such payments, the mortgagee shall comply with the following requirements:

1) Prior to filing a Motion for Relief, the mortgagee or its agent shall review the Trustee's website to verify it has received all of the payments reflected therein; and

2) If, after review of the Trustee's website, the mortgagee determines there still exists a default in the ongoing mortgage payments, it may proceed with the filing of the Motion for Relief.

4) Secured Claims and Valuation of Collateral Under 11 U.S.C. § 506.

A) *Secured Claims to Which § 506 Valuation is NOT Applicable.* The amount listed in the "Claim Amount" is the amount proposed by the Debtor in the Plan. If the actual allowed claim is different from the amount specified and the Trustee determines that the Plan will still complete as proposed, the Trustee shall pay the actual amount of the allowed claim without the need for an Amended Plan.

B) *Secured Claims to Which § 506 Valuation is Applicable.* The amount of a secured claim to be paid under this Plan is the lesser of the amount listed by the Debtor as the "Value" and the allowed secured portion of the holder's claim. If the Court orders a different amount than is shown, the Plan shall be deemed amended without the requirement of the filing of an Amended Plan unless the Trustee objects that the Plan will not complete as proposed. Any amended plan thereafter must use the amount ordered by the Court.

5) Separately Classified Claims. This section deals primarily with the Co–Debtor's claims and is otherwise self explanatory.

6) Executory Contracts And Unexpired Leases. This section is self explanatory.

7) Priority Claims. Anytime a domestic support obligation (DSO) exists (even if the Debtor is current on payments) the DSO claimant must be listed in both the Plan and on Schedule E. The amount listed as the "Estimated Arrearage" is the arrearage amount proposed by the Debtor in the Plan. If the actual allowed claim is different from the estimated arrearage amount and the Trustee determines that the Plan will still complete as proposed, the Trustee shall pay the actual amount of the allowed claim without the need for an Amended Plan. If the Debtor is current on his or her DSO obligations then he should make an "X" under the word "Current."

If the Plan addresses a DSO assigned or owed to a governmental unit under § 507(a)(1)(B), the Debtor should use section 7(B) of the Plan. If the Debtor proposes to treat this claim as a general unsecured creditor pursuant to § 1322(a)(4) then the Debtor should so indicate by inserting the word "NONE" under the language "Est. Amt. Paid." If so treated, the Debtor must also propose a Plan that satisfies the requirements of § 1322(a)(4).

Secured Income Tax Claims and 11 U.S.C. § 507 Priority Claims. This section is self-explanatory.

8) Long–Term Debts Paid Outside by the Debtor or Co–Debtor. This section is self-explanatory.

9) Avoidance of Liens. This section is to identify creditors against whom the Debtor is proposing to either avoid or reduce their secured lien pursuant to law. This section does not constitute a judicial determination of whether these actions are allowed under the law.

10) Unsecured Claims. This section is designed to set forth the minimum amount the Debtor must pay to allowed general unsecured creditors pursuant to sections §§ 1325(a)(4) and 1325(b).

11–19) These Sections are Self–Explanatory.

20) Reason(s) for Amendment(s). This section requires a brief, concise statement setting forth the reasons for any amendments of the Debtor's original Plan. The failure to complete this section on all Amended Plans will result in the Amended Plan being noticed as deficient by the Clerk's office. If there is a substantial change to the proposed Plan payments or upon the Trustee's request, the Debtor shall file an amended Schedule I and J.

PART THREE—Additional General Requirements for All Cases Filed on or After August 1, 2011

In addition to any duties imposed by law, rule or order, the Debtor must also perform the following duty concerning insurance on motor vehicles in Chapter 13 cases:

1) Insurance on Motor Vehicles in Chapter 13 Cases.

A) *Required Coverage.* The Debtor in a Chapter 13 case shall maintain full-coverage insurance on any motor vehicle on which a lien exists to secure a debt, naming the lien holder as an additional loss-payee. The Debtor shall provide for a collision and comprehensive deductible of not more than $500.00. If the security agreement or other contract requires a deductible lower than $500.00, such contract will govern the amount of deductible the Debtor is required to maintain during the bankruptcy case.

B) *Proof of Insurance Coverage.* The Debtor in a Chapter 13 case shall provide the lien holder with proof of insurance providing full coverage, as listed in paragraph (A), from the date of the bankruptcy petition. If the insurance policy lapses during the pendency of the case, the Debtor shall be required to provide new proof of coverage which shall include proof of three months prepaid insurance. A copy of the policy or the policy declaration sheet and a copy of a receipt or similar payment statement from an insurance agent on company letterhead may be used as proof of coverage if the documents verify the terms of coverage and pre-payment of premiums.

Appendix A

Rights and Responsibilities of Chapter 13 Debtors and their Attorneys

It is important for those who file a bankruptcy under Chapter 13 to understand their responsibilities, as well as those of their attorney. As such, this document sets forth the services required to be performed by your attorney, as well as those responsibilities that are required and/or expected of you. In order to maintain a high standard of quality for the Debtors' counsel practicing in this district, the following requirements are mandatory for the Debtors' counsel in a Chapter 13 bankruptcy. These requirements are in addition to any others required by law, rule or order. Should a conflict arise between these rights and responsibilities and any law, rule or order, the law, rule or order shall supersede the conflict. Notwithstanding the foregoing, no provision, statement and/or clause contained herein shall be deemed as a limitation on the Debtors' counsel's responsibilities and/or obligations as set forth in the Bankruptcy Code.

Before the bankruptcy petition is filed, the attorney will provide the following legal services:

1) The Debtor shall meet with an attorney for a reasonable period of time prior to the filing of the bankruptcy petition to review facts and to receive advice concerning the Debtor's bankruptcy and non-bankruptcy options and shall be present at the signing of the final documents.

2) Unless an emergency filing is necessitated by exigent circumstances, the Debtor's counsel must collect the following documents from the Debtor prior to filing, or document the inability to collect the same, subject to subparagraph (*o*) below:

a) Copies of all bank account statements (or similar documentation) from at least 60 days prior to the date of the filing of the bankruptcy petition (savings, checking, CD's etc.).

b) Federal income tax returns, transcripts, or a completed affidavit declaring that the Debtor was not required to file tax returns for the tax year prior to the filing of the bankruptcy petition.

c) Federal income tax returns, transcripts, or a completed affidavit declaring that the Debtor was not required to file tax returns for the second through fourth years prior to the filing of the bankruptcy petition.

d) A copy of all payment advices or other evidence of payment the Debtor received within 60 days before the date of the filing of the petition from any employer of the Debtor, or an affidavit that no income was earned.

e) A copy of all payment advices or other evidence of payment the Debtor received within the six calendar months prior to filing the petition sufficient to calculate the Debtor's current monthly income pursuant to § 101(10A).

f) If the Debtor is self-employed, a profit and loss statement for the six months before the filing of the petition.

g) Copies of all billing statements for the Debtor's credit cards, medical bills, student loans, personal/payday loans, car loans, mortgages and other secured debts. Also, any utility bills on which the Debtor is *not* current. If the Debtor does not have a bill for a debt, the Debtor must provide a written statement of the (i) creditor's name, (ii) billing address, (iii) account number and (iv) amount owed.

h) A copy of any domestic support order that the Debtor has been ordered to pay.

i) Copies of final and signed divorce decrees and marital settlement agreements entered into in the two years prior to filing the bankruptcy petition.

j) Copies of any and all documentation concerning lawsuits or administrative proceedings the Debtor has been involved in within the last two years, regardless of the status or outcome of the suit.

k) If applicable, a statement from the county showing the current status of the Debtor's real estate/mobile home taxes. If the taxes have been purchased, the Debtor should provide a copy of the redemption certificate.

l) Copies of the most recent non-term life insurance statements in which the Debtor has an interest.

m) Copies of current statements regarding any non-retirement investments in which the Debtor has an interest.

n) Verification/information of the balance of any and all 401(k) loans.

o) If any of these documents are not available or present in the Debtor's counsel's file, then the Debtor and the Debtor's counsel should execute an affidavit stating that they both made reasonable efforts to obtain the documentation and were unable to comply. The affidavit must also list the documents not obtained.

3) The Debtor's counsel must complete an intake document which is reasonably detailed to ensure that the Debtor is asked the appropriate questions and given appropriate advice. There is no form intake document approved by the Court at present.

4) The Debtor's counsel must ensure that the Debtor has completed the required pre-petition credit counseling requirements or determine if the Debtor meets the standard for one of the exceptions to such requirements.

5) The Debtor's counsel must review the petition, schedules, supplemental local forms, Chapter 13 Plan and mailing matrix prior to the filing of said documents.

6) The Debtor's counsel must meet with the Debtor when they sign the final paperwork to be filed in their case.

7) The Debtor's counsel must review and sign all motions filed in the Debtor's case.

8) The Debtor's counsel shall timely provide the Debtor with a written executed contract that conforms to the requirements in the Bankruptcy Code and Rules.

After the bankruptcy petition is filed, the attorney will provide the following legal services:

1) Upon information received from the Debtor, take steps necessary to avoid the termination of, or to allow the reinstatement of, the Debtor's necessary utility services by providing faxed proof of filing of the petition to utility service creditors.

2) Take steps necessary to obtain the return of repossessed vehicles, which are necessary to the estate, including, but not limited to, the filing of Complaints to Compel Turnover.

3) In the event of pending state or federal court litigation, notify creditor's attorneys and the appropriate court in which the litigation is pending that the bankruptcy case has been filed.

4) Send out an information letter to the Debtor reminding the Debtor to attend the § 341 meeting, specifying the time and location of that meeting, and advising the Debtor as to the procedures of the § 341 meeting.

5) Appear at the § 341 meeting of creditors with the Debtor, confer with the Debtor to prepare him or her for the § 341 meeting, and advise the client to cure any arrears on Plan payments. Counsel will appear at all meetings dressed in professional attire.

6) Upon information received from the Debtor, take steps necessary to terminate pending wage garnishments, including filing a Motion to Terminate Garnishment.

7) Attend all court hearings relating to the Debtor's case, excluding adversary proceedings in which counsel is not retained.

8) Prepare and conduct all court mandated pre-trial conferences, reports, briefs, etc.

9) Address objections to Plan confirmation and, where necessary, prepare an Amended Plan.

10) Prepare, file, and serve necessary modifications to the Plan, which may include suspending, lowering, or increasing Plan payments.

11) Prepare, file, and serve necessary amended statements and schedules, in accordance with information submitted by the Debtor, provided the Debtor pays the Court's filing fee, unless the amendment or omission was due to the fault of Debtor's counsel.

12) Prepare, file, and serve necessary motions to buy, sell, or refinance real property when appropriate.

13) Review all proofs of claims filed and, if appropriate and in the Debtor's best interest, object to improper or invalid claims.

14) Timely file proofs of claims for creditors who fail to file claims if it is in the Debtor's best interest to file such a claim.

15) Represent the Debtor in motions for relief from stay and file an objection to such motions, if appropriate.

16) Where appropriate, prepare, file, and serve necessary motions to avoid liens on real or personal property.

17) Upon information received from the Debtor, contact creditors who continue to communicate with the Debtor after filing, by phone or in writing, and, if necessary and appropriate, file motions for sanctions, prepare testimony and exhibits, and appear for hearing.

18) If necessary, contact tax authorities or other third-parties to gather information necessary for the case. However, such contact shall not include the obtaining of the names, addresses, account numbers and other information necessary for the inclusion and filing of creditors on any schedule of the petition, as it is the duty of the Debtor to provide such information to counsel for the preparation of accurate bankruptcy schedules.

19) These rights and responsibilities do not include a requirement to represent the Debtor in an adversarial proceeding and the Debtor's attorney may require additional fees which must be approved by the Court.

20) Communicate with the Debtor—either by phone or by being available for office appointments—to discuss pending issues or matters in the present case.

21) Provide such other legal services as, in the attorney's sound judgment, are necessary for the prompt administration of the case before the Bankruptcy Court. Nothing contained herein shall be construed to bind the attorney to perform work that has no basis in law or fact or constitutes extraordinary proceedings within the context of a normal chapter 13 proceeding, such as adversary proceedings or other work that exceeds the scope of the attorney-client contract.

The requirements for payment of attorney's fees in Chapter 13 cases for the Southern District of Illinois provide for a flat-rate attorney fee of $4,000.00 for a non-business related Chapter 13 bankruptcy and $4,500.00 for a business bankruptcy as defined in § 1304, or for payment based on regular billing. Fees shall be paid through the Plan as provided for by the Confirmation Order. The attorney may receive part of the allowed fees prior to the filing of the case for the actual services performed prior to filing, provided said fees are deducted from the total allowed fees as paid through the confirmed Plan. The attorney may move to withdraw or the client may discharge the attorney at any time. The attorney agrees to perform substantially all duties designated above. If the attorney does not substantially perform all of the above duties inclusive, then, upon filing of a motion and after a hearing before the Court, the Court may order the attorney to disgorge all or any part of the fees received, as the Court, in its discretion, deems appropriate. If the case is not confirmed, then the attorney is allowed only those sums as set forth in the Chapter 13 Procedures Manual.

In addition to those duties and responsibilities set forth in 11 U.S.C. § 521, the Debtor(s) shall:

1) Keep their attorney informed of their current mailing address and contact information (including home, work and cell phone numbers). If the Debtor is proceeding pro se, the Debtor shall file a Notice of Change of Address with the Court.

2) Timely make all payments as called for by their Plan, whether through a wage deduction or directly, as set forth in the Plan.

3) Immediately notify their attorney of any wage garnishments or attachments of assets which occur or continue after the filing of the bankruptcy case.

4) Notify their attorney upon the loss of employment or other financial problems that may arise.

5) Notify their attorney if they are sued or contacted by a creditor (or a creditor's agent) after the bankruptcy case has been filed.

6) Contact their attorney before buying, refinancing or selling any real property or before entering into any long-term loan agreements to determine what steps must be taken to obtain the required approval for same.

7) Cooperate with their attorney in the preparation of all documents and attend all hearings, if required. This obligation includes timely responding to all letters and phone calls left by your attorney.

8) Comply with all other additional contractual obligations and terms with your attorney as specifically set forth in your attorney-client contract.

Dated: _____   _____
                                  Attorney for Debtor

Dated: _____   _____
                                  Debtor

[Effective August 1, 2011. Revised December 1, 2011; June 1, 2015; July 21, 2015.]